F. W. Harris.

St. Catherine's.

SOME PROBLEMS
IN ETHICS

First published 1931
Second impression, corrected, 1933

SOME PROBLEMS
IN ETHICS

BY

H. W. B. JOSEPH, M.A.

Fellow of New College and late Lecturer
in Philosophy in the University of Oxford,
Fellow of the British Academy

OXFORD UNIVERSITY PRESS

OXFORD UNIVERSITY PRESS
AMEN HOUSE, E.C. 4
LONDON EDINBURGH GLASGOW
LEIPZIG NEW YORK TORONTO
MELBOURNE CAPETOWN BOMBAY
CALCUTTA MADRAS SHANGHAI
HUMPHREY MILFORD
PUBLISHER TO THE
UNIVERSITY

*Printed photographically from the sheets of the First Edition
in Great Britain by* LOWE & BRYDONE PRINTERS LTD.,
LONDON, N.W.1

PREFACE

THE following chapters are in substance the same with a course of eight lectures delivered at New College in the Lent Term of 1930. These were not written with any idea of publication; but if I say something about how they came to be given, it may explain both why they are now published and certain other features of the book, besides an amount of iteration more defensible in lecture than in book form. In palliation of this, I can only say that I am not sure that I could have performed upon my children, any more than she did, the promise of Medea.

For a number of years past, many of us whose studies lie in philosophy at Oxford have been perplexed by the difficulties connected with obligation. We have discussed it much among ourselves, and it has been painful for some of us to find how little we know. The interest in the problem has been reflected, not only in the Lecture-Lists but in several published works. I may mention, besides some referred to in the text, Professor Prichard's article in *Mind* in 1912 (N.S. xxi, pp. 21–37), under the title 'Does Moral Philosophy rest on a Mistake?'; Professor G. C. Field's *Moral Theory*: though this was not written in Oxford; and Mr. W. D. Ross's *The Right and the Good*, which unfortunately only appeared after my proofs had been corrected. The course of lectures to which I have referred was an attempt to get down on paper the best answer I could give to some of the questions concerned: with whatever little success, to straighten my own mind.

For this reason the lectures dealt, and the book deals, rather freely and by name with the published views of some of my colleagues here, as well as of distinguished writers elsewhere. But I had to be guided by a knowledge of what works were most likely to be familiar to an audience to be drawn from the two schools in which Moral Philosophy finds a place in Oxford. Merit and familiarity explain also why certain writers are specially quoted among the famous dead. I was as it were intruding into a discussion, and had to address myself to the remarks of the other speakers whom the audience would have already heard.

That the issues are of a difficulty that many treatises on Ethics insufficiently appreciate, I make no doubt. If I should make only that plainer to some than it has been before, I should not think the publication of the book wholly unjustified. I do not profess to be fully satisfied with the solution offered; it is the best that I can find. Should I in anything said have misrepresented the meaning of any writer quoted, I express my regret, and would ask the reader, neglecting to whom they are imputed, to treat the opinions discussed as the subject of his reflection, and consider only what in them is true.

H. W. B. J.

Oxford,
October 1930.

CONTENTS

ERRATUM

Page 15, ll. 17–18 : *for* it is inconsistent with there being
knowledge, or even true opinion.

read it is inconsistent with there being
knowledge—even knowledge that
there is a distinction between true
and false opinion.

I

ETHICS AND NATURAL SCIENCE. METAPHYSICAL PRELIMINARIES

THE questions with which Ethics is concerned suggest themselves to men's minds, when they reflect upon their own and others' conduct, and upon the judgements which are passed on conduct. But answers to these questions cannot be found without reference to what answers we make to another set of questions—those that arise in reflecting on the world in which this conduct belongs, our claim to know it for what it is, and its relation to ourselves who know it.

In particular, Ethics must make its account with what may be called the scientific theory of the world; whether all men of science hold this theory true does not here concern us. On this theory, it is their investigations which discover to us what the world in which men live and act really is; men are themselves just a part of this world; the laws discovered to be exemplified in the events of this world are the laws exemplified also in the events which make up the histories of men, who are but items in its contents. This theory, pushed to its consequences, raises many difficulties for Ethics. It is inconsistent with the freedom of men's actions, in any sense in which they have been held to be free. It is equally inconsistent with any real unity of a self. The Behaviourist school of psychology has perhaps made the most persistent effort of late to push the theory through regardless of paradox. As psychologists, the writers of this school claim to be investigating conduct, but to dispense with introspection in doing so, and to study the soul as 'objectively' as one might study the movements of plants. Not the thinking which we are

B

pleased to suppose expresses itself in our actions, but the
bodily movements or behaviour in which it is said to
express itself, is what psychology should concern itself
with; the very word 'behaviour' is chosen because less
likely to suggest, as 'action' might, something different
from what occurs in a physical system physically determined. That a man thinks is that a certain series of
changes in his brain is initiated by a stimulus from outside
it, and in turn initiates or discharges itself into slight
incipient motor reactions in his larynx; that he speaks is
that this series of changes is prolonged into larger movements of the larynx and movements of other organs of
speech imparting certain vibrations to the air; that he acts
is that the series of changes in the brain discharges itself
into determinate movements of the limbs. That as a
result of experience he thinks or speaks or acts differently
from how he would have done without such experience is
that the stimuli constituting the experience have led to
certain changes in his body in virtue of which it is otherwise disposed than before the experience occurred, so that
now stimuli initiate changes in his brain or receptor nerves
that issue in different movements of larynx, vocal parts, or
limbs from what would have ensued, had the same present
stimuli fallen upon his body as originally disposed.

The fundamental principle involved in this account is
that of what is called the 'conditioned reflex'. A well-
known experiment with dogs makes its nature clear. A dog
naturally, i.e. in virtue of its congenital physical organization, salivates at the scent of food; that is an ordinary
'reflex action' (the word 'action' is to be understood here
in the same sense as when we speak of the action of the
heart or of a safety-valve, and not as when we speak of
moral action). It requires us to admit, for its explanation,
the existence of nothing but bodies and the laws in accord-

ance with which they change position relatively to one another. Now if, when food is placed within smelling distance of a dog, and so near enough for the olfactory particles to reach the nasal passages in numbers sufficient to stimulate to the reaction of salivating, a bell is at the same time rung in the neighbourhood, a definite stimulus of the dog's auditory nerve will accompany the olfactory stimulus that naturally provokes the salivatory reflex; and when this has happened a number of times, it will come about that the auditory stimulus, without the olfactory, will provoke the same reflex. You may say, if you like, that the dog salivates at the mere thought or imagination of food, instead of at the smell of it. But there is no need to introduce into the explanation anything so unobservable as thought or imagination. We need only grant that the repeated conjunction of the two stimuli, auditory and olfactory, so modifies in the dog's cerebral cortex the resistances between the centres these stimuli excite, and also between them and those involved in the motor response of salivation, that now the excitement from without of the auditory centres alone will touch off the centres for the response.[1] Thus the salivation occurs as a physical change in accordance with physical principles; all that has

[1] In *Gestalt* psychology, for this mechanical description is substituted a theory of what is called dynamical development in a total brain field. But tendencies in experience are supposed to be physiologically determined by the properties of the dynamical processes in the brain. I do not therefore see that the substitution is of any importance in regard to the philosophical issue here raised. The distinction between the workings of machines and of dynamical systems insisted on by Köhler (*Gestalt Psychology*, ch. iv) seems to me a distinction between one kind of mechanical process and another, unless he thinks that a dynamical process is purposively directed. But this he would appear to regard as 'unscientific', rightly.

to be has been accounted for. Sensation, thought, imagination *may* occur; but in our explanation of the animal's behaviour they can be left out. What we *must* acknowledge, however, is the conditioned reflex, since otherwise the reaction cannot be explained on physical principles at all; and unless we so explain it, we cannot bring the movements of matter which are the salivation within our scientific scheme.

Now there is no difference in principle between salivation in a dog and his snapping, eating, barking, pursuing, or caressing. All are movements of matter: of those particles of matter which make up the body of the dog, or rather, the body called the dog. The parts involved in these movements can all be set moving by appropriate stimuli in virtue of the physical constitution of the body called the dog, and the disposition of that body's parts; though constitution and disposition have been modified from what they were at birth by past stimuli, of light and air, warmth and food, and by the reactions of the body to them. And if there is no difference in principle between salivation in a dog, and his snapping, eating, barking, pursuing, or caressing, equally there is none between those in a dog and crying, seizing, eating, speaking, pursuing or otherwise behaving in a man. There are differences of complexity between the systems of linked receptor and motor centres involved in dog and man, but that is all. In the man as in the dog, the principle of the conditioned reflex, together with the congenital disposition of bodily parts, and the laws exemplified in modification under stimulus, is adequate to account for all behaviour. It may be easier for us to offer explanations of human conduct in terms of desire, imagination, thought, purpose, hope, disappointment, means and end, and so forth. But that is because we are ignorant of what is occurring in the cortical, neural, and muscular structure involved in the behaviour which we are in the habit of explaining by reference to those other ineffective factors. They are ineffective because they are quite heterogeneous with both stimulus and response. But these are matters of scientific observation; they are movements of bodies; they have their place in the physical order, and are linked according to the laws exemplified there with the rest of the movements of these and the other bodies which together constitute the physical world. How can any one who consistently holds the view of what really is and happens taken in the scientific theory of the world suppose that the stimulus and the response, movements of bodies in space and time, are connected in any other system than that which science investigates? How can desire, thought, purpose, and so forth connect the stimulus and the response, unless they too are bodies or movements of bodies? The Behaviourist would have no objection to bringing them into his account, if they are such; but then in observing the changes within the body that intervene between stimulus and response, we shall be observing desire, thought, purpose. On this view, the incipient laryngeal movements which occur when we think but do not speak our thoughts *are* our thinking, as those of lips and tongue in which they issue when we speak our thoughts are our speaking; and introspection is as little necessary to the study of thought as to that of speech. It informs us of nothing really operative in or necessary to the process connecting stimulus and response, but at most of that from which we may conjecture something about this process that would otherwise remain concealed from us.

Let me attempt by a comparison to bring out what this position comes to. Suppose we could construct a railway-system—the scale does not matter—with a switch-mechanism whereby as the trains run over the lines they set the points for themselves before reaching them, or for other trains after; and with a more intricate apparatus, to be carried no doubt partly on the several carriages or trucks (which might have independent motors), whereby these coupled or uncoupled themselves as they moved, and were redistributed about the system. Fresh carriages inserted into the system would modify the behaviour of those already in it, and this would show itself by the passage of carriages outside some central area of the system when otherwise they would have remained within that area. Let the main part of the switch-mechanism and other fixed apparatus lie within the area in question. An observer wishing to understand the movements of carriages outside it, and why they pass its barrier-limits when and where they do, assembled as they are, and with the velocities they have, should observe how the lines run within it, and the mechanisms there, whether fixed or on the carriages. But he might be precluded from doing this, and only able to observe the lines, points, carriages, and coupling apparatus on carriages, outside the barrier, within which when the carriages pass they are beyond his ken. Let us, however, further suppose an electric apparatus connecting all points and pieces of coupling apparatus with an indicator-board outside the barrier and open to observation, so that whenever anywhere a carriage passes any points, or engages or disengages with another carriage, some corresponding sign is shown on the board. An observer precluded from following the movements of the carriages within the barrier, if he could read the indications on the board, might learn that something was happening to the carriages between the times when they entered and left the barred area, and even from a study of the points and the coupling apparatus on the carriages outside it conjecture the mechanisms within, and finally explain in terms of these why the entry of certain carriages within the barrier was followed by the exit of those or others at such and such places and times. But the indications on the board would be no part of the process constituting the working of the railway-system, and tabulinspection (if I may so denominate studying the readings on the board) would not perceive its working. The system itself would be an object not of tabulinspection but of train inspection. If you like to say that part of what you watch on the board *is* movements of carriages inside the barrier, you may equally say that another part of what you watch on the board is movements of carriages outside the barrier. And with the same degree of justification the Behaviourist may say that thinking is laryngeal motion.

Something like this identification of the readings on the indicator-board with the working of this supposititious railway-system is involved in holding that the conduct reflected on by a moral philosopher, and the judgements about such conduct that he reviews or makes, are really a part of what happens in the physical system, which in our scientific studies we take for real. Some who, like Mr. Russell in this country, are sympathetic to Behaviourism, depart from the lines of my illustration in an important respect. They hold that the perceiving mind is in large part a series not of states in the perceiver's body, nor of states whose objects are states of other bodies, but of those changing states of other bodies themselves. Only it includes besides, or there attach themselves to the grouping of these Janus-faced states which belong to the histories alike of what we call a mind, and of what we call bodies and objects of the mind, certain other states, such as thoughts and imaginings (or, better, images), of which no account need be taken when we investigate the laws of physics—

i.e. the laws exemplified in those series of states which the physicist regards as belonging to or making the being of the various bodies in the world; but account must be taken of them, as well as of states belonging to the physical series, when we investigate the laws exemplified in the groupings and series of states that make the history of what we call minds. These laws are psychic laws; the others are physical. That is physical which obeys the laws of physics, and that is psychical which obeys the laws of psychology; but some terms, which we may call sensa, or perhaps also feelings, occur in the series illustrating laws of both kinds; the New Realists call them 'neutral stuff'. The neutral stuff, and the elements of mental imagery (if we allow, against the Behaviourists, that the latter also exist) together make up what is real. Physics and psychology investigate each a different set of groupings and relations among these elements of the real. But though the laws exemplified in the two sets of groupings are not the same, the scientific attitude is the same in investigating both; so that physics and the study of mind do not in principle differ otherwise than do any two particular sciences, such as chemistry and physiology.

It seems clear that, if all this were true, what each of us calls *himself* would be no genuine subject or unity; his so-called actions would be groups of 'neutral' or imaginational items not states of any subject or unity or self; no change or happening would be *his* action, and no praise or blame could be imputed to any *him*. In short we should have on this theory to say that ethical doctrine was all error, if it were not that on the same theory there would be no one to err, and neither error nor truth.

It would be beside our purpose to dwell further on the implications of Behaviourism, or of Neutral Monism. The second is an explicit metaphysic, the first a psychology resting on a metaphysic to whose existence and implications it is equally blind. They illustrate, in the results which their acceptance would have on ethical theory, how its problems cannot be pursued alone. But they have not the prestige of the strictly scientific standpoint. From their assumptions their exponents have not, like the men of science from theirs, deduced numberless consequences applicable in practice to the improvement, and sometimes to the destruction, of man's estate. These applications to practice incline us to accept the scientific standpoint as true; and yet, if this standpoint is to be taken in regard to all that happens in the world, it too leaves no room for a conduct that is other or more than responses to physical stimuli, whether provided for in the 'agent's' body at birth or conditioned by changes stimulated in it since.

So long as we are content to treat our scientific assumptions about the nature of the world as true, when explaining events not ascribed to human action, and to ignore them when they collide with the account of some of these events given in an ethical theory that treats them as the acts, or due to the acts, of a moral agent, we may talk the language of physics in the laboratory, and that of ethics in the law-court or the pulpit. But so long also the position of an ethical theory is altogether precarious. When the questions with which it deals have once set us reflecting we must ask whether the assumptions which we make in answering them are consistent, not only with the facts that they are to explain and among themselves, but with what else we take for true. Not only, e.g., must we ask whether the freedom which we ascribe to a man when he acts is consistent with his being able to act otherwise, or with blaming him for acting as he does, or with blaming others also for his so acting; we must ask besides whether it is consistent with the physical theory that connects the movements in his action, say of forging a cheque, with other movements of bodies in an unbrokenly determined series that contains no subjects of praise or blame. For the true account to be given of anything, whether the forgery of a cheque, or the growth of a plant, or the fall of a stone, is one account. It was not the best of the schoolmen who drew the distinction between what was true for faith and what was true for reason, and taught that the same doctrine could be true for one and false for the other. In their own minds most, I think, of those who drew it either rejected the faith which they dared not openly deny, or mistrusted the reason which they yet could not but use as if they trusted it. And no more to-day can a reasonable man, when he has started on questioning any of his beliefs, and their consistency with what else he knows and believes, draw a line between one portion of them and another, and say that he will make consistent only with what falls on one side of the line his answers to his questionings.

Many philosophers have seen the necessity of this policy of Thorough, and, indeed, it is the very business of philosophy to pursue it. And some in the pursuit of it have thrown overboard ordinary ethical beliefs, as Hobbes did,[1] and with less clear-sightedness certain biologists who thought the theory of evolution as competent to explain man's mind as his body.[2] Others have attempted to replace the ordinary assumptions of physical science by assumptions more or less shocking to science and to common sense: like Berkeley, or Leibniz, or (shall we add?)

[1] Hobbes's account, *Lev.* i. vi, of 'the interior beginnings of voluntary motion; commonly called the Passions' is not really very far from Behaviourism.

[2] e.g. T. H. Huxley, who held that if evolution showed the groundlessness of moral distinctions, it was our duty to tell the truth and say so.

T. H. Green. Kant thought that he had found a *via media*, and that he could justify himself in using in the laboratory the assumptions of Newtonian physics, but as an educationist those of Ethics, because men and their actions belong to two orders, the phenomenal and the noumenal. I do not think his attempt to establish this position succeeds.

What, then, of what we have been accustomed to believe or think we know, can we retain, and what must we abandon when we set out upon an ethical inquiry? When we ask ourselves this, we notice at the outset that in each set of doctrines, ethical and scientific, are included statements which at first sight we are inclined to say we know to be true: such as that there is obligation, and ability to discharge it, on the one hand, and that all events in nature conform to some law on the other. Yet the two seem incompatible. This must lead us to hesitate before we accept as knowledge what we are inclined to take as such. No doubt there are starting-points of knowledge, ἀρχαὶ ἐπιστήμης, which we know but cannot prove; but we are apt to take as evident what, when challenged, is found not to be so. It may be that when, as we must if challenged, we consider it again, we do find that to be evident which before we thought so. It may be that we find it after all doubtful. Then we must ask how far it fits in with other principles, known, or accepted though doubtful. For my part, I should say that the principle that in whatever happens the succession of events conforms to a rule according to which the earlier determines the later, is of the latter sort. We think it true, because we are thinking only of what happens in a mechanical system, of inertial bodies interacting according to laws. In such a system there is neither development nor purpose. If development does anywhere occur, or there exist purposive changes, the changes belonging to the course of the development or purposively sustained exhibit successions that cannot be understood on the principle that the earlier determines the later according to a rule. It does not seem to me that purposive activity is less intelligible than mechanical determination; indeed the second is less intelligible, the more closely you scrutinize the assumptions which it requires to be made. The mathematics in mechanical explanation is so clear that the understanding of that betrays men into thinking they understand the physical principles as well. If you once grant that the energy in one body can be transferred to another, but that energy itself can be neither created nor destroyed, you may proceed contentedly with your equations; but you are no nearer understanding what it is for energy to be transferred from one body to another, nor indeed what energy is, or its relation to body, nor therefore how it is a quantity at all. The supposed presumption, therefore, in favour of the self-evidence of the 'principle of uniformity' or of mechanical determination being removed, it remains to ask whether we know anything to be true which is inconsistent with the complete mechanical determination of all changes that occur in bodies.

And here we have to admit the success of the efforts of men of science to exhibit the physical world on this assumption as an intelligibly connected system, and the shattering effect which the denial of the correctness of the assumption at any point has upon their whole conception of the nature of the real. It was for this reason that Kant held it for so great a merit in his philosophy, that it reconciled, by the distinction of *homo phenomenon* and *homo noümenon*, the freedom of the will in moral action with the complete mechanical determination of all events in nature, including those bodily movements in which a man's free choice

expresses itself when he acts. Leibniz indeed had made
the same claim. He held that all which a man did pro-
ceeded freely and spontaneously from his own nature, and
yet that with sufficient knowledge we could account upon
mechanical principles for all that happened in the phenomenal order, including even the writing of the books that
were written.[1] Neither claim, I think, can be substantiated.

But if so, and if we had no call to question the truth of
scientific principles except in the interest of maintaining
that of conflicting ethical principles, I think many would
be inclined to drop the latter—to treat moral distinctions
as pointing to nothing real beyond modes of feeling and
believing which arise under certain conditions in men's
minds. There is, they might say, no *knowledge* of good and
evil, right and wrong, because nothing that happens really
is any of these. There is only a discoverable connexion of
events really happening and producing consequences, with
feelings of pain and pleasure and the use of certain words,
including words such as 'approval' and 'disapproval', to
signify these feelings and their connexion with what produces them. Not every one would be satisfied with this
account; some, upon the best consideration that they could
give to the question, would say that this was not what they
meant when they said of anything that it was good or evil,
right or wrong, that men ought or ought not to do certain
actions; that in so speaking they recognized something for
which if an account of the real left no room, it could not be
correct. But others would dissent, and that without self-
contradiction.

[1] Cf. a passage printed by E. Bodemann, *Die Leibniz-
Handschriften der kgl. öffentlichen Bibliothek zu Hannover*, p. 89,
quoted by Höffding, *History of Philosophy*, i, note 75; E. T. i,
p. 518. That all events admit of mechanical explanation as well
as of one from final causes Leibniz repeatedly asserts.

If, however, the principles underlying the scientific account of what the world really is, and how what really happens in it is related to what passes in the minds of men, were as little consistent with maintaining the distinction of truth from error as with maintaining that of good from evil or of right from wrong, then however shattering to the sufficiency of this account may be the denial that these principles are altogether true, I see no alternative to denying it. For the scientific account, though not claiming to be good or right, claims to be true; and it cannot reasonably do this, and abolish the possibility of knowledge.

Yet surely it does abolish this possibility. In the extreme instance of a Behaviourist account of the mind, that seems obvious; for if thought *is* laryngeal motion, how should any one think more truly than the wind blows? All movements of bodies are equally necessary, but they cannot be discriminated as true and false. It seems as nonsensical to call a movement true as a flavour purple or a sound avaricious. But what is obvious when thought is said to *be* a certain bodily movement seems equally to follow from its being the effect of one. Thought called knowledge and thought called error are both necessary results of states of brain. These states are necessary results of other bodily states. All the bodily states are equally real, and so are the different thoughts; but by what right can I hold that my thought is knowledge of what is real in bodies? For to hold so is but another thought, an effect of real bodily movements like the rest. An intelligence not determined by what falls within this bodily system to which belong the conditions producing our thoughts might, if it were capable of knowing both the events in that system and the thoughts of it which these determine, discover under what conditions bodily events within the system produce thoughts of it agreeing with what this extraneous intelligence knows it to be, and under what conditions not. But the thought determined by these conditions could not know what the extraneous intelligence knew without being itself also extraneous to the system within which, nevertheless, the conditions determining it are supposed to lie. These arguments, however, of mine, if the principles of scientific theory are to stand unchallenged, are themselves no more than happenings in a mind, results of bodily movements; that you or I think them sound, or think them unsound, is but another such happening; that we think them no more than another such happening is itself but yet another such. And it may be said of any ground on which we may attempt to stand as true, *Labitur et labetur in omne volubilis aevum.*

That the principles, then, on which rests the scientific theory of the world are absolutely true is not only inconsistent with ethical theory; it is inconsistent with there being knowledge, or even true opinion. And therefore with themselves; for they claim to be matter of knowledge, or at least of true opinion. Since that is so, we are not required to make our ethical theory consistent at all points with the scientific account of the world; if our ethical theory is to be true, it must not be built upon the principles of the scientific account, or require their unquestioned acceptance. And this result, if correct, is of importance, and illustrates the necessity to Ethics of a metaphysical foundation.

II

SOME CONFLICTING OPINIONS

THAT freedom and duty, good and evil, right and wrong cannot be set down *a limine* as words standing for nothing real, on the ground that no room for their application is to be found in the account of what the real is which is given us by physical science, is all that has been established so far. New difficulties arise when we ask for what they do stand, and how these matters are related.

To many it has seemed that good and evil are the most fundamental matters with which Ethics is concerned. A well-known ethical treatise of recent years is called *The Theory of Good and Evil*.[1] Professor G. E. Moore[2] reduces ethical questions to three. The first is, 'What is meant by *good*?' And the answer to that is that it cannot really be answered, for good is indefinable: it is 'a simple, indefinable, unanalysable object of thought', by reference to which the subject-matter of Ethics must be defined.[3] The second question is, 'To what things in what degree does this predicate directly attach? What things are good in themselves?' And the third is, 'What causal relations hold between these and other things?' For according to Professor Moore (and he says it is obvious) to say that conduct is right or obligatory at any time is to say it is the conduct by adopting which more good or less evil will exist in the world than if anything else were done instead.[4] But he does not seem to think that Ethics is called upon to consider the meaning of the word 'obligatory', though different views have been held about its meaning; and

---

[1] By the late Dr. Hastings Rashdall.
[2] *Principia Ethica*, § 24, p. 37.
[3] Ib., § 15, p. 21.　　　　　[4] Ib., § 17, p. 25.

some have asked whether the conduct which to Professor Moore is obviously obligatory is so when the agent will himself suffer injury by it, or (as it is said) when it will not be for his own good. To which Professor Moore would reply that 'his good' is an improper expression [1]; what is good is just good, whether it be also mine or also some one else's; and to one's obligation to adopt on any occasion that course of conduct whereby more good or less evil will exist in the world than by the adoption of any other, it is irrelevant whose the good is to be: just as if it were obligatory to adopt that course whereby more cats would exist in the world than by adopting any other, and it was irrelevant who was to own the cats. But here not all agree with Professor Moore. To Plato also it seemed obligatory to bring in some sense into existence what was good, but also that so far as a man did what he ought, he made the good his own possession; and this fact could not be separated from the obligatoriness of the conduct. Many have agreed with Plato in this matter. And yet Kant altogether dissevered the consciousness of obligation from any consideration of the interest or advantage of the man obliged [2]; and Professor H. A. Prichard has recently maintained very strongly that Kant is correct, and that the failure to dissever them gave rise to an *ignoratio elenchi* in the argument of Plato's *Republic*. Socrates is there represented as undertaking to refute the contention of Thrasymachus and others about justice. They contended that certain actions ordinarily *thought right* or obligatory are not so, because not to the agent's advantage. Socrates should have pointed out that 'the question whether some action which men think just will be profitable to the agent has really nothing to do with the question whether it is right.' Instead, he tries to prove that *right* actions are profitable to the agent.

[1] Ib., § 59.   [2] Or thought he did; but cf. *infra*, pp. 108–11.

Plato does not notice that this is not a refutation of the sophistic contention; for the Sophists held that the actions in question could not be known to be right except by proving them to be to the agent's advantage, whereas Socrates treats them as known to be right *ab initio*, and their advantageousness as a further fact about them. Plato wished to prove this further fact because he passionately wanted men to do right, but believed they could only act from desire of their own good. Had he realized the falsity of this belief, and that whatever it is that renders an action a duty, it is not conduciveness to one's own good, he would not have been involved in his *ignoratio elenchi*.[1] Further, in a point where Professor Moore dissents from Plato, Professor Prichard dissents from both. Not only is Plato mistaken in holding that in doing what I ought to do, I seek my own good; Professor Moore is mistaken in holding that in doing what I ought to do, I need bring into existence something good at all. There is no necessary connexion between doing what is right and bringing into being what is good except this, that doing what is right is itself good when I do it because I think it right.[2] What is right need not be causally related to any good.

The severance of right from good has been expressed in another way; a right act, it has been said, merely as such, has no value in itself. The doing of it may have value; if the motive to doing it is the thought of the act's rightness, or (some would say) the desire to do right, then it has; but there are motives to doing it which would make doing it positively evil. But the right act considered in itself is of no value [3]; and the world is neither a better nor a worse

---

[1] *Duty and Interest*, pp. 5–21.

[2] *Mind*, N. S. XXI (1912), pp. 25, 30.

[3] Cf. W. D. Ross, *Proceedings of the Aristotelian Society*, 1929, p. 252: *The Right and the Good*, pp. 132–3.

place for its being done; and this apparently in spite of the fact that it is my duty to do it.

Again on the one hand it has been widely held that action is rational or intelligent just in so far as the agent is moved to act as he does by the conviction that in so acting he realizes or brings into being some good; on the other, according to Kant, to act rationally is only to act from a sense of obligation; it is *quâ* rational that a man is conscious of obligation, but the obligation of which as rational he is conscious is not to pursue or bring into being any good, but to find a principle of action which he and other rational beings placed in his situation might, in the consciousness each that the rest were adopting it, all adopt without self-contradiction or self-stultification, and himself now to act accordingly. But writers of yet another way of thinking reject both these views of the function of reason in acting, or of what distinguishes the action of rational beings like men from that of other members of the animal world. Hume held that reason is and ought only to be the slave of the passions [1]; though if it is, what he meant by adding that it ought to be is not clear; perhaps that results such as men like are better secured by its being so than if it were not. In any case my being rational neither determines in any way what for its own sake I desire, nor provides a spring of action other than desire and capable of rendering a desire ineffective.

This opinion is shared with Hume by Professor McDougall, in his *Introduction to Social Psychology*. The intellectual processes, he says [2], are but the servants, instruments, or means used by us in the service of a number of impulses or instincts that are congenital in man and are the sources of all energy. These primitive instincts or

---

[1] *Treatise of Human Nature: Of the Passions*, Part III, sect. iii.
[2] Loc. cit. (20th ed. 1926), p. 3.

tendencies, the motive powers of all thought and action, 'are the bases from which the character and will of individuals and of nations are gradually developed under the guidance of the intellectual faculties'.[1] An instinct is an innate specific tendency of the mind, common to all members of any one species, that has been slowly evolved in the process of the adaptation of the species to its environment [2]; and that can neither be eradicated from the mental constitution of the individual in which it is found, nor acquired by the individual in its lifetime.[3] It is psychophysical (though what that means is not very clear); and it 'determines its possessor to perceive, and to pay attention to, objects of a certain class, to experience an emotional excitement of a particular quality upon perceiving such an object, and to act in regard to it in a particular manner, or, at least, to experience an impulse to such action.'[4]

All action then is accounted for by instinct; and an instinct is provoked into energy by the perception of something. To judge something good is not to perceive anything, so that on this view, if it be held consistently, it cannot be the judgement that anything is good which determines action. Neither is the consciousness of obligation an instinct, nor, therefore, a motive power of thought or action. Reason, says Professor McDougall, cannot

[1] *Introduction to Social Psychology*, p. 17.

[2] I suppose that for an instinct to have been slowly evolved cannot in this context mean more than this: that in a series of individuals connected by descent different forms of instinct are found, but that these can be arranged in an order of approximation to the form of instinct found in members of the present generation, and that so arranged they are in the same order as if arranged chronologically. At least, if it does mean more, I think intelligence would turn out to have been somehow at work in the evolution of the instinct.

[3] *Introduction to Social Psychology*, p. 20.   [4] Ib., p. 25.

create desire [1]; and it is not apparently in virtue of being rational that we desire anything—a position perhaps not quite the same as that reason *creates* desire. 'The function of reason is merely to deduce new propositions from propositions already accepted.' [1] It is true we have been told that from the bases of these instinctive tendencies 'the character and will of individuals and of nations are gradually developed under the guidance of the intellectual faculties'. But it is possible 'to exhibit human volition of the highest moral type as but a more complex conjunction of the mental forces [2] which we may trace in the evolutionary scale far back into the animal kingdom'.[3] The complications of the instinctive processes are indeed great, 'so great that they have obscured until recent years the essential likeness of the instinctive processes in men and animals'.[4] It is also true that every instinct is modified by experience.[5] But it is hard, I think, to see how this modification should amount to more than an alteration in the specific response to the stimulus constituted by the perception of some object, or an attachment of the response to stimuli by which it was not originally provoked.

But Professor McDougall's list of the principal kinds of complication of instinctive response that occur takes us a good deal beyond this. For we are told that finally 'the instinctive tendencies become more or less systematically organized about certain objects or ideas'.[6] The meaning

---

[1] Ib., pp. 325–6.
[2] i.e., the innate tendencies to react to the perception of some particular object by feeling a particular emotion and performing a certain action.   [3] *Introduction to Social Psychology*, p. 15.
[4] Ib., p. 27. Yet one reason given by Plato for distinguishing 'spirit', τὸ θυμοειδές, the instinct of pugnacity, from the rational, τὸ λογιστικόν, is that the first is found in animals, and not the second.   [5] Ib., p. 27.   [6] Ib., p. 28.

of this is obscure; but it would seem to be something very different from any mere conjunction of particular impulses to respond by definite actions to definite stimuli, even with emotions thrown in. We must not forget that each instinct is a distinct spring, so that the number of them can be given.[1] No doubt several may be excited together, and one can understand how, if the excitation of a particular impulse can come to attach itself to a new stimulus, the same stimulus may come to excite more than one. It might be as with an organ. There are stops that set each a different range of pipes into action, and stops that set into action several ranges at once.

What, however, could be the guidance of the intellectual faculties in this development among the instincts? No doubt it occurs in building an organ. It should, I suppose, lie in settling what complications of instinctive process shall be formed. But if so, the intelligence must proceed either by way of ascertaining how to achieve a particular complication which already, independently of intelligence, is desired; or by way of conceiving such complication which thereupon is desired; or in both ways. But it cannot proceed in the first way, without the second; for it cannot ascertain how to achieve that of whose nature there is no conception. And if it proceeds in the second or in both ways, the conception of something by the intelligence gives rise to a desire, and so intelligence would be, or help to constitute, a spring of action. But the only springs of action are our primitive instincts, severally or in combination. Each of these determines its possessor to perceive an object of a certain class, and respond to the perception of it with a particular emotion and action in regard to it.

[1] Professor McDougall's original list contained twelve. In his latest edition he expresses himself more doubtfully about their number: *v.* pp. 386 sq.

Now a desire to achieve a particular complication of instinctive impulses, however much our intellectual faculties may guide us in achieving that complication when once we desire it, cannot itself arise within the scheme of this psychology. For this allows no sources of energy in the mind except so many distinct but complicable instincts. Each instinct is aroused by the perception of some object. A complication of instincts is not an object of perception; it cannot stimulate to activity an instinct or complication of instincts; the desire to achieve it cannot be an expression of any one of the instincts whose complication is desired, nor of their complication. Though our intellectual faculties therefore might work in the service of this desire when once it had arisen, yet, unless they can give rise to it, it cannot arise. But accordingly to this psychology they cannot give rise to desire. The spring of action therefore required, if we are to suppose that some systematic organization of 'the instinctive tendencies . . . about certain objects or ideas' is to arise under the guidance of the intellectual faculties, is, on the principles of this psychology, one for which neither our instincts nor our intellectual faculties can account, and so one which cannot exist in us.

If, then, the character and will of individuals and nations (supposing a nation to have a character and will, as well as an individual) are gradually developed merely from the basis of twelve or more innate instinctive tendencies, it cannot be under the guidance of the intellectual faculties; for these can only guide us in action to which there is already an innate instinctive tendency in the mind. There is no such tendency to achieve a certain complication of instincts, and therefore no intelligently guided action achieves it. If it comes to be, it is a mere result of the several instinctive tendencies working together, as the accidents of the occurrence of stimuli may determine. It is no more intelligently guided than the often lamentable results of the pushings of a number of people, each without regard to the rest, to get out of a burning building by the same door. The particular complication of dead and living bodies that comes about on such an occasion was neither desired nor intelligently guided. And so, as far as I can see, and as, I think, Plato saw long ago when he wrote the fourth book of his *Republic*, must it be in the development of character and will, if that psychology is true for which there are signs, in Professor McDougall's opinion[1], that it 'will before long be accorded in universal practice the position at the base of the social sciences which the more clear-sighted have long seen that it ought to occupy.'[2]

It would be absurd, of course, to dispute the importance of a sound psychology in studying the questions that belong to Ethics, for many of them are questions about what goes on in a soul. But the psychology which claims to be a science like other particular sciences, and to go its way as independently of metaphysical questionings as they do, is as little entitled to put forward its results as something with which ethical theory must nowhere come into conflict as they are. We must ignore the results of neither, particularly not those of the physical sciences; for the success with which they account for so much of what happens in bodies is enough to show that something very near the principles from which they proceed is true; whereas the principles from which what claims to be a

[1] *Introduction to Social Psychology*, p. 2.

[2] I hasten to add that there is much in Professor McDougall's later work, inconsistent as far as I can see with it, to which I attach a far higher value than to what I have been criticizing. But I am not sure that there is much to which he does.

scientific psychology proceeds are often (as in a particular instance I have just tried to show) by no means successful in accounting for some very important things that appear to happen in souls, like the development of character and will. Still, psychology also has its successes, as in the treatment of mental disorders, which are to be acknowledged with respect and gratitude; and although I think that in some respects the success reaped in practice is independent of the psychology supposed to justify it, in others it implies the truth of assumptions about the soul which are of real importance to ethical theory.

The disagreements then that reveal themselves among those who have attended to the theory of conduct are extensive; and here this is particularly disconcerting. For though Ethics, like any other study, is an attempt to know, the questions to which it seeks answers are often put in the interest of practice. In a sense Aristotle was mistaken when he said of his *Ethics* that it aimed not at knowledge but at action. Immediately, it aimed at knowledge. But the knowledge is desired by men in doubt how to act. οὐ γὰρ περὶ τοῦ ἐπιτυχόντος ὁ λόγος, says Socrates in the *Republic*, ἀλλὰ περὶ τοῦ ὅντινα τρόπον χρὴ ζῆν: 'we are discussing no casual subject, but how a man should live.' [1]

One can perfectly well imagine that in an age and country where men were all agreed how they should live, they might reflect on what was implied about themselves and the world by the fact that they ought to live thus. But in history and fact ethical speculation has been provoked by the doubts men have come to entertain about the truth of traditional opinion on how they ought to live. And these doubts, and the great discrepancies not only among opinions entertained in different places before reflection,

[1] *Rep.* i. 352 D.

where custom was followed unquestioned, but also among the conclusions reached by men when they have reflected, must make one diffident in claiming truth for propositions in this field which at times one is tempted to call self-evident. I do not say that it has no self-evident propositions; and of course 'self-evident' does not mean evident at once, or to all. But I find myself accepting much which is not so, as what, where I have not reached knowledge, seems to me nearest the truth.

Let us, therefore, examine some of the discrepancies of view above rehearsed with this chastened hope of a decision. We may begin with the problem not of good, but of right. A right act, some say, is not to be defined as one causally related to what is good; and it may have no value in itself; nevertheless, I ought to do it. In spite of the arguments by which this position has been defended, it seems to me absurd. Why ought I to do that, the doing which has no value (though my being moved to do it by the consciousness that I ought, has), and which being done causes nothing to be which has value? Is not duty in such a case irrational? It is admitted that the goodness of my acting from a sense of duty cannot be that which makes the action what I ought to do; but I am told that it is the nature of obligation to be thus ultimate.

I own that I am not content. Yet neither does the utilitarian position, which finds good only in that to which right acts are causally related, content me. For is there no intrinsic goodness in acting rightly? It is the conviction that there is which gives its impressiveness to the ethical doctrine of Kant, who insists on this so strongly.

It is this difficulty, how to reconcile the conviction that the obligation to do an action does not arise merely from the goodness of some results or consequences of the action, with the conviction that the action that I recognize I ought to do cannot be without value in itself: how to maintain that obligation is neither derived from the goodness merely of the consequences of the action to which I am obliged, nor yet independent of relation to any goodness, that will be seen to provoke most of what attempts to be constructive in the present discussions.

III

RIGHT ACTS AND MORAL ACTS

WE are to consider what distinction should be drawn between a right and a moral act: an act which *is* right, and one *done because* it is, or at least is thought to be, so; and whether it is true that whereas a moral act always has value, being an expression of a good will, a right act may have none, and the world, if it was not done because it was thought right, be none the better for it, although still it is what the agent ought to have done. I have said that to me this seems *prima facie* not true.

Let me state here by way of anticipation what I propose to argue for. An act may be right because productive of good results, and a man, knowing this about it, may see in this the reason why he ought to do it; if, seeing this, he does not do it for that reason, he will not be acting morally, and there are motives which would make his act immoral; nevertheless, the act would, in a defensible sense, have been right. An act may also be right not because productive of good results; but if so, it must have intrinsic goodness, which goodness must involve the agent's motive. It is here that the heart of the difficulty lies. For a man ought to do that act in which he recognizes rightness; but a character of an act that involves his motive in acting cannot, so the argument runs, make the act what he ought to do. For his motives at a given moment are not in his power. It may then be his duty to act in a certain way, but it cannot be his duty to act from a certain motive; for what I cannot do, that it cannot be my duty to do.

I believe this argument not to be fatal, and that its plausibility springs partly from concentrating our attention too much on the goodness of acting from what may be called the sense of duty as such, in contrast to that of acting either from a sense of the duty to do actions of some definite sort, as to keep promises, or to help our neighbours, or from desires of certain sorts; partly from overlooking a peculiar difference between the sense of duty and other kinds of motive.

Our present business, however, is to get the distinction between a right and a moral act clearly before us. A hungry man, finding food, if no reason occurs to him why he should not eat, will do so; a kindly man, finding a child in distress, similarly will try to comfort it; an enthusiastic archaeologist, finding what look like worked flints, similarly will examine them. These actions are done from particular desires, or instincts if you will, without reflection or consideration; not, therefore, because doing them is thought for any reason good, nor from a sense of duty. Nevertheless, doing them may be good, so that the agent, if anything led him before acting to consider whether he should do them, would recognize this goodness, and do them because of it: or again, if what checked him was a desire towards some other action which he saw to be incompatible, might do them because he thought he ought.

In recognizing such goodness, there need be no question of means and end. Eating when one is hungry no doubt maintains one's strength, and might help a man to finish a journey; the maintenance of his strength, or the completion of his journey, is something to which eating is a means. But one may think eating good, when one is hungry, apart from any such results desired. It is true that all that is in a man's power is to ingest the material; if for any reason it should fail to nourish, it will not satisfy his hunger. But it would be a mistake to oppose ingesting food, and satisfying his hunger, as means and end. There is no thought of such a causal relation in a man's mind. His action is eating to satisfy hunger. So a man who tries to comfort a child does that for its own sake. He might do it in hope to gain the affections of its widowed mother; then we might properly distinguish trying to comfort the child as means, from that as end. But supposing he does it for its own sake, to comfort the child, a distinction between means and end within his action is mistaken. For this distinction is between an action, and some consequence which it is hoped will follow, but without which there would still have been the action. Now if the distinction is pushed back within an action done for its own sake, the element distinguished as means is a mere movement of the limbs, κίνησις τῶν ὀργανικῶν μερῶν, as Aristotle expressed it; and that is not, in any sense with which Ethics is concerned, an action. The minimum action is doing this or that to satisfy one's hunger, to comfort the child, to discover if the flints are worked.

Particular actions such as these may be done without reflection; or they may be done because a man thinks he ought to do them. It is not contended that a man who, when considering what he ought to do, judges some particular action to be right, judges without regard to any specific character or particularity in it. That would be impossible. The act which is, or which he thinks, right must have a character in virtue of which it is or is thought to be right, if he is to distinguish it as right from other possible actions, and so decide the question what he ought to do. But it is contended by some that this rightness is neither being causally related to anything good, nor any kind of intrinsic goodness. If it were either of these, a man doing the act because he thought it right would act with reference to a good other than what lies in acting from a sense of duty: whether to a good consequential on the act, or intrinsic to it. He would thus at once act morally,

because acting from a sense of duty (and to act so is good);
and he would have done a right act, because of a goodness
consequential or intrinsic to it. And this latter goodness,
though not the former, would come into being through his
action, should he do the same act not from a sense of duty.
It is this latter goodness which, when intrinsic, I have said
must be connected with the nature of his motive. If then
his motive is not a sense of duty, yet it must not be a bad
motive; if it were, the act would not really have been the
right act, that which the man ought to do. Those whose
contention I am traversing say that it would. Its rightness
belongs to an action, on their view, because of its specific
nature; but that nature need neither lie in its being causally related to any good consequence, which would be the
utilitarian position, nor be good itself. Therefore the act
may be right and have no value, and the world not better
and even (because of evil consequences) worse for the
coming into being of the action, except so far as, if it be
done from a sense of duty, the world is better for that
expression of a good will.

Though, if this is the consequence to which the distinction
leads between a right and a moral action—between doing
what is right and doing it from a motive which makes the
doing good—one might well wish to reject the distinction, it
is easy to see how we are led to make it, and indeed find it
difficult to avoid. A man who asks himself in some actual
situation what he ought to do, and proceeds to do what
upon consideration he thinks he ought, would be said both
to have done what he thought right, and from a good
motive. But might he not do the same act from a bad
motive? Let us suppose a man X employed in some
position of trust, the Secretary let us say to a Colonial
Governor, but also an intimate friend of another man Y
living in the Governor's jurisdiction. Y reveals to X, as

between friends, and after letting him know that he relies upon their friendship for the information he would give him to be treated as confidential—perhaps after first securing from him the assurance that he might so rely—a scheme that he is hatching which the Governor, if he knew of it, would undoubtedly hold it his duty to prevent. He reveals the nature of the scheme to X finally, let us say, by letter, and on the very eve of its execution, so that X may be unable to demand release from his promise to treat the information as confidential before imparting it to the Governor, if this is to be done in time for the execution of the scheme to be stopped. In such a situation X might well hesitate about his duty, especially if he himself thought that the execution of the scheme would bring on balance great advantage, and that the Governor, though bound, if he had wind of it, to stop it, would not be sorry that it should have been executed without his getting wind of it. Now let us suppose that upon consideration X decided that it was right to reveal to the Governor what he had learned; and let us assume further that in this he was correct. He clearly would not think that it *was* right *because* he thought so; for then it would equally have been right to keep Y's communication secret, if he had thought that. But he had asked himself which of two incompatible courses was right; the two possible answers are mutually inconsistent—whichever is true, the other is false; and no one, asking himself which of two inconsistent propositions is true, can think that which is true depends upon his answer. If then the right action in this situation is to tell the Governor, it is so whether X does tell the Governor or not, and therefore, if he tells him, for whatever reason or with whatever motive he tells him, it is still right.

Let us then next modify our imaginary illustration and suppose that X, placed in this situation, had asked himself not what he ought to do, but what it would pay him best to do; and that having first resolved to keep silence in the belief that the scheme would succeed, and that Y would put him in the way of very lucrative work in consequence, he found reason at the last moment to change his mind about the prospects of the scheme's success; and thinking now that it would anyhow fail, he divulged it to the Governor in the hope of official promotion. He would still, it may be said, in divulging it, have done a right action, but no longer one morally good. He would only have done a morally good action, or acted morally, had he divulged the scheme because he thought he ought to.

But why, if the right act were in itself without value, and the world in no way a better place for its being done, should X judge that he ought to do it? There is no difficulty in allowing that to act from a sense of obligation is good; but is there none in an obligation to realize what is in no way good? The conviction of difficulty here has led many to say with Professor Moore that a right act is always causally related to something good. Such rightness would belong to an act independently of the motive from which it were done; and in that sense, though not in the sense that its rightness was irrespective of the goodness of its consequences, the act might be called right in itself. In so calling it, I should be making an assertion of the same sort as in saying that rain would improve the crops. At a given time and place this might be true, whether or not rain were coming, and whether or not it were in any one's power, and, therefore, any one's duty, to do anything which would cause it to come. So, whether or not there is any one able in a given situation to perform some act, it might still be true that it would cause more good than any other that could be performed in that situation, and so was right in itself. We can give a meaning on these lines, as Utilitarians, to the statement that an act is right in itself, though I doubt if it is what those who use the phrase would have expected to find themselves meaning. But perhaps they might add that they had not hitherto considered the matter with enough care.

On this view then an act is to be called right by reference to the goodness of the results which it would cause: obligatory, however, only upon some one able to perform it. There may be no one able to perform it, and yet it remains true that it would, if performed, produce those good results. Provided then that we may speak as if an unperformed action were something to which predicates belong at all, we can call the act right in itself and without regard to any person who ought to perform it; but we cannot so call it obligatory. To put the point otherwise, it is a person who ought to do the act, it is the act which is productive of good results. The act, therefore, is right in its character as an event, or change in the physical order; the doing of it is obligatory not as this change, but as the bringing about of this change. And this bringing about of the change, it will be noted, is not another change in the physical order preceding and determining the act in its character as an event. It is something to which a place cannot be assigned in the physical order at all, though occurring in the same time in which physical events occur. And that the doing of the act is obligatory is a statement still unprecise. It is obligatory, if at all, only upon some one both able to do it and knowing that relation of the act to resulting good which is meant by calling the act right. We speak more precisely, therefore, when we say not that doing the act is obligatory on X, but that X ought to do the act. When we put it that way, it is easy to see that his knowledge, or at least his belief, of the causal relations in virtue of which the act is right is as necessary, to *his* being obliged to do it, as are the causal relations themselves; indeed we should probably say that his belief of the causal relations, without the relations themselves existing, would be enough to create an obligation on him. Obligation, on this view, though directly an obligation to do the act which is in a man's power, and which is not good, arises in virtue of his belief in some result which is good to be expected from the act, and for whose coming to be, however it came, the world would be the better. Obligation, therefore, does not arise, or does not exist (as the admission that a right act had no value in itself threatened to require us to allow) independently of relation to anything good.

This reasoning seems quite satisfactory so far as it goes; and it goes far enough to cover many cases where a man asks himself, in some actual situation, what he ought to do. But it does not seem to cover all cases, nor perhaps the first form of that imagined above. For it was there supposed that X believed that the consequences of Y carrying out his scheme without the Governor getting wind of it would be on balance good, and yet was correct in deciding that he ought to divulge it. The reader may refuse to allow that such a decision would have been correct. A consistent Utilitarian would certainly refuse. But we shall be forced to condemn as erroneous many judgements that almost everybody would in fact, in various historical or hypothetical situations, make, if we are to recognize no obligation to do any action that does not appear likely to produce consequences on balance better than those of any available alternative.

It will be argued later that in such cases there is a good to be looked to, which in a sense is beyond the action, but yet not as are its consequences.[1] Meanwhile in distinguishing as above between the obligation on a man to do

[1] Cf. *infra*, p. 73, and ch. viii.

an action, and the rightness of that action in itself, we still have not resolved the difficulty that we found in the distinction of a right and a moral act: viz., that though this distinction is one which it seems necessary to accept, it implies that obligations can arise in no relation to anything good.

IV

ACT AND MOTIVE

THE position we have so far reached is this. We ought to do certain actions because they are right. That does not mean, because we ought to do them; what then does the action being right mean? It might mean that it is causally related to something good; but if, as we have held, we ought to do some actions of which that cannot be said, then there must be a rightness which is not being causally related to something good. Now could we include in what we call the action some motive, being moved by which, or the manifestation of which, is good, then there would be a goodness *in* the action, which might be the reason why we ought to do it. But this it is said we cannot do; our motives are not at our command, as that must be which we ought to do. The right act, therefore, is just doing something, not doing it from a certain motive. Indeed from whatever motive a man does what is right, it is still what is right that he does. I ought to pay this debt, because my paying this debt is right; and whether I pay it for that reason, or (if it is not the same) from a desire to do what is right, or because I am fond of my creditor, or because I dislike my heirs, or for fear of legal proceedings, in any case I do what is right in paying it. And in my paying the debt from some of these motives there would be no value; and the results of the transfer of wealth involved may be on balance bad. The motives to the act and the results of it may be good or bad; the act itself is neither. It is of a definite sort, determinate, but without value. I ought to do it because of its determinate nature, not because of any value that it has.

I wish to suggest that these right but valueless actions do not exist. A right act would presumably be still an act. The epithet 'right' is not presumably intended to cancel the proper meaning of the noun 'act' in respect of what is called both act and right, as, when one spoke of a forged Raphael, the addition of the epithet 'forged' would be meant to cancel the ascription to Raphael of the picture which is called both a Raphael and forged. But no act exists except in the doing of it, and in the doing of it there is a motive; and you cannot separate the doing of it from the motive without substituting for action in the moral sense action in the physical, mere movements of bodies. The motive of course need not be the sense of obligation.

It will, perhaps, be retorted that there may be actions without a motive, in the sense of the word 'action' which concerns Ethics. The action of the heart no doubt is not action in this sense. But consider some action such as is generally done with a motive, but may on occasion be done from force of habit. A man, say, has got into the habit of locking his roll-top desk before leaving his room; we should not think that a man ordinarily ought to do this, but there is no harm in it. If, however, he had a number of confidential papers on his desk which he ought not to give any one else a chance of reading, then it would be his duty to lock his desk before leaving his room. Now he may lock it from force of habit, without thinking about the papers; if so, he certainly has not done a moral act. But has he done a right act? I think not. He would have done a right act, if remembering the papers, and that he ought not to leave them about, or remembering them and wanting to keep them secure because they were confidential, without explicit consideration of any obligation, he had locked them up. But that did not happen.

No doubt the key was turned in the lock, and the papers

thereby so placed as to be physically concealed from prying eyes. But we cannot describe an action, as it concerns Ethics, in mere physical terms. If what is real is barely the world about which physical science informs us, a world to which it is indifferent that any one is aware of it, then there are no actions in the real world. Movements of my body, like those of any other body, belong to physics, not to Ethics, and are neither right nor wrong. It would not be accurate to say that action is merely in the mind. A man who locked up confidential papers to prevent unauthorized persons reading them would be acting in turning the key. I do not think we can defend the view that there are two systems, a mental or psychical and a physical, that moral action occurs in the first, and right action in the second, and that they have a certain correspondence; nor yet that both moral and right action occur in the first, and determine or are accompanied by the same event in the second. The world in which men act, rightly and wrongly and perhaps in ways to which neither qualification belongs, is the world which they in part perceive and know. Their actions take effect in this world, or (better) work in it; for to say that they take effect in it might suggest that they occur in one order, the psychical, and their effects in another, the physical; and that the two are related in the external manner of the cow and the dog, when the cow tossed the dog that worried the cat, and the cow's action took effect in the dog's transit through the air. It would be a nearer comparison to say that an action works in the world in which we act, as ambition works in a man's mind, or oratory in an assembly. None of these comparisons is exact, for the relation of mind to nature is not that of different factors within the unity of one mind, nor of different persons to one another in an assembly. But when we speak of ambition working in the mind, we do not think that ambition and the mind are two things separable from each other as are a cow and a dog, coming into a conjunction to which (though not to its results) their natures are indifferent; nor are the minds of an orator and of his audience in spatial externality, nor as disparate as the life of a mind is from what physical science treats the world as being. Of the relation of mind to nature it cannot be said that any wholly satisfying account has been suggested. We have to ask meanwhile, for what must an account find room, and not jettison it, if it is to satisfy us. It seems to me that so long as we hold the world and what happens in it really to be what physical science treats it for, we cannot talk the language of Ethics, and must jettison conduct.

If then one day a man locks confidential papers in his desk automatically, and another day in order that unauthorized persons may not get at them, the two actions do not differ only numerically. The physical relations of papers and desk-top and lock-bolt and key may be the same each time, and the events as physical science studies them may differ only numerically. But these must be regarded in Ethics as so related to the different actions that they cannot be really separated from them. They come about through them not as the dog's transit through the air comes about through a toss of the cow's head, but as speech comes about through thought. The man who cried Caunian figs, CAVNEAS [1], as Crassus started on the ill-fated expedition which ended in his death at Carrhae, was not warning him not to go. Had some one so warning him uttered the 'same' cry[1], the cries, however as sounds they might have been capable of being confused, would as cries not have been the same; for you cannot separate their being as cries from the thought expressed in them.

[1] CAV(E)NE(E)AS.

The relation of thought to the language in which it finds expression (and it may express itself in other sensible forms than language) is indeed, as the omen on Crassus' march shows, such that there is no necessary connexion between a particular thought and particular sounds, though when certain conventions are established, the expression of our thought must conform to them. And the relation between an action which can be right or wrong and the change of arrangement among bodies in which the action expresses itself is to some extent also a matter of convention; so that the same moral purpose or action can express itself in different 'outward acts', or different in the same, according to institutions and usages holding in different communities. I do not wish to stress this comparison of the places of convention in the two fields. But I would stress the comparison between our thought expressing itself in speech, and our action expressing itself in the movement of our limbs, or for that matter of other bodies under our control. Both the 'outward act' and speech, which is indeed a sort of outward act, can be regarded from the standpoint of science as just movements of bodies, but you can no more treat the act as that in ethics than speech in logic. And there is no more, it seems to me, a right act except as it is the expression of a motive which makes it also either a moral or at least a virtuous act, than there is a true statement except as it is the expression of the thought of some one thinking truly. You cannot really put away a lot of truths in a book-case.

I would like to suggest as a matter for consideration whether the theory of propositions at one time held by Professor Moore and Mr. Russell does not involve the same sort of mistake as the theory that makes a right act something independent at once of motive and result, distinct from an act moral or virtuous. Propositions, by that theory, are distinguished alike from existing things and from statements or the judgements these express. They are objects of thought and study, with definite relations, discoverable by us, one to another. They are in themselves true or false, the truth of a proposition consisting in a specific relation of it to existence. To me it seems that there are no propositions, in this sense, any more than there are right acts of no value. When I know, or come to a certain opinion, I express my knowledge or opinion in a form of words which I call a proposition. My knowledge is of, or my opinion concerns, a reality which is independent of my knowing it or thinking thus about it; although I do not believe either that there is a real world independent of mind altogether, or that my mind is independent of that mind of which the world is not independent. The relation of the knowing mind to what it knows is not one of accidental conjunction. But besides the knowledge or opinion that expresses itself in a proposition there are other activities of mind, like wondering, supposing, and considering (as we do in logical discussion) particular instances of knowledge or opinion and their kinds, affirmative or negative, and so forth. Now in these cases, though I am not myself as it were bringing to birth a knowledge or opinion expressing itself in a proposition, I must still use the propositional form. Hence I come to think of a proposition as something detached alike from knowledge or opinion in me, of which, when I really propound it, it is the expression, and from the reality which I should be knowing, or about which I should be having an opinion, if I were propounding it. Thus some have come to suppose that there are propositions waiting as it were to be known, considered, supposed, and so forth: as independent of knowing, considering, supposing them as what exists is; which, therefore, may be said to be or subsist without existing, and to be by themselves true or false. Whereas really it is only thinking which is true or false, unless knowing, which of course cannot be false, may properly be called true; and propositions are called true or false as they express thinking.

So, when I act, my action may be right or wrong. But I have occasion to consider actions which I am not performing, as I may consider a knowledge or opinion which I am not bringing to be in my mind. There is the world in which I act, to which also belong the objects of my knowledge or that with which my opinion is concerned. This world I treat as something independent equally of my awareness of it and of my acting in it, except that I do alter it by my action and not by becoming aware of it. But besides it, and my actions in it, there are 'actions' which I barely consider; which are neither changes which I effect in it, nor my effecting those changes, as those *soi-disant* propositions are neither what I become aware of in it nor the expression of my awareness. Not being done, those 'actions' are yet called right and wrong, as those propositions are called true or false. And if they were at all, they would be capable of these differentiations. But no action is, except in being done, as no proposition is, except in being reached in thinking or re-thinking. And when the actions are done they are done with a motive.

I submit then that there is no action in which we must not include a motive: at least none that concerns Ethics. If we are to call action the execution of certain movements from mere force of habit, as when from mere force of habit I lock my desk before leaving my room, that sort of action perhaps does not include a motive. Analytic psychology has shown that there may be a motive, without one's being conscious of it. What is most important about the discoveries of this psychology, I would say in passing, in a speculative and not a therapeutic interest, seems to me commonly ignored: viz. that the mind works purposively at lower levels than is commonly thought. In consequence they do not make it easier to apply to those psychic activities which psychology studies the methods of physical science, which take no account of purpose, but harder. But I do not raise here the question where, or whether anywhere, a line is to be drawn between action which is part of conscious behaviour and action which is part of conduct. I would only urge that if anything belonging to the first is to be called an action, like the instance above taken, yet it is not a right action. In what belongs to conduct, to speak of an act merely as such and not as including the motive is to suppose that you can abstract from an act something essential to its being, and yet that there would be an act left, only devoid of this element; as if one spoke of a body merely as such and without its extension, or of sovereignty merely as such and without its unity, or of a line merely as such and without its continuity, or of action again merely as such and without its freedom (if those are correct who say that an unfree act is a contradiction in terms), or of a conspiracy merely as such and without the common purpose which makes it criminal or lawful. For a conspiracy is a common purpose working itself out through divers persons into a change in the state of things; and an action is one man's purpose working itself out through him into a change in the state of things. Take away the common purpose, and there is no conspiracy, and nothing lawful or criminal; take away the single man's purpose, and there is no act, and nothing right or wrong.

V

SOME OBJECTIONS CONSIDERED

IN the present chapter certain objections will be considered which might be or which have been brought against the position maintained in the last.

(1) The same act, an objector might say, may surely be done from different motives; and therefore the act must be something, irrespective of the motive. But are they really the same act? Different acts, having different motives, may work themselves out into the same movements of bodies; but these are not the acts. A man who was fond of oysters might eat a plateful put before him for the sake of their flavour; a man who loathed them might do so to avoid hurting his host's feelings; a man who loathed or was indifferent to them might do so to prevent his neighbour, whom he knew to be fond of them and he disliked, from having two portions. I think these are three different acts, one morally good or else kindly, one morally bad or spiteful, one indifferent. They are not three instances of one act, viz. eating a plateful of oysters. One might do that in one's sleep, or absent-mindedly: would those be two more instances of the same act of eating a plateful of oysters, three of the five having motives and two not, but all five, as instances of the same, being irrespective of motive? What is left, if you take away the motive, is conscious behaviour like that of animals, whom, when Aristotle said that they did not act, πράττειν, he did not, like Descartes, think to be unconscious automata. Whether there be not, in some animals, the germ of action proper, I do not discuss; but if there be, the instances of it are not behaviour and something besides, an undeveloped motive; the behaviour is no longer itself just the same.

And so an act proper is not analysable into behaviour and motive; it is indivisible. You cannot conceive that the motive might be taken away and the behaviour left really the same; though a man may sink from a level at which he acts to one at which he only behaves, as he may pass into a second childhood.

So one man may believe and another know demonstratively that the side of a square is incommensurable with the diagonal; but the latter's knowledge is not belief *and* a demonstration, nor can the knowledge be deprived of its demonstrativeness and the belief be left; though a man who did know by way of demonstration may cease to do so, and revert to belief. One man's knowledge and another man's belief, or the same man's knowledge at one time and belief at another, may express themselves in the same statement. But that does not make the statement expressive of the same act of thought, irrespective of differentiae of belief or knowledge, nor therefore, in a logical regard, the same proposition. And if it be objected that not the proposition but the demonstration, with premises and conclusion, is the proper expression of his thought who knows the side of a square to be incommensurable with the diagonal, we may take some different example, where the proposition is necessary but not demonstrable, though it may be believed by those who do not understand the necessity: as that quantity is infinitely divisible. The difference here between knowledge and belief is only the more notable.

(2) A second objection to the position I wish to defend is, it will be remembered, that it cannot be my duty to do what is not in my power to do; it is not in my power to feel a particular motive which I am not feeling, nor therefore to act from it.

(*a*) It may, however, be a man's duty to act in accordance with the promptings of a particular motive which he does feel. A man who judges that he ought to do some act because it is right must have a sense of obligation; but he may at the same time be inclined to the act by some motive like gratitude, or affection, or benevolence, and its involving this motive may be what, in the situation in which he is placed, makes the act right. Thus, if I am prompted or inclined by affection to do some kindness that will cost me money, and simultaneously by desire for amusement to spend the money on myself, I may judge that I ought rather to do the kindness; and the rightness because of which I judge that I ought to do it is its having the goodness that lies in its being an expression of affection, the alternative action, which is an expression of the desire for my own amusement, having thereby an inferior goodness or none at all.

If I were passing judgement upon the action of another man who in such a situation had done the act of kindness, whether merely because the desire to do it was stronger than and suppressed his desire to amuse himself, without any consideration or choice, or because upon consideration he so preferred, I should think better of him than if the relative strength of his desires, or if his preference, had been the other way, although he had never asked himself which he ought to do, nor therefore been moved by a sense of duty; he would not have acted morally, but his act would have been right, and that because of his motive. Similarly, if he had not yet acted, I should judge that he would be acting rightly, if he should do the act of kindness. And equally when my own prospective action in such a situation is in question, shall I not find a rightness in *my* doing what I should find a rightness in *his* doing? This rightness is a kind of goodness which the act would have, even if done without any thought that I ought to do it, and would have because of the motive involved. But if I hesitate whether to do the act to which affection prompts me or to seek instead my own amusement, and my hesitation is resolved by the sense that I ought to do what is right, then I shall have acted morally as well as rightly. Thus in cases like this I can distinguish the rightness of the action that consists in its being one where the impulse of affection is preferred to or prevails over one of self-indulgence from my obligation to do it because of this rightness.

(b) On the other hand I may have no kindly or other good impulse; and then the act cannot owe its rightness to being a manifestation of a better choice or better impulse. Nor can the act owe its rightness to being a manifestation of that sense of duty to which it owes its morality. When looking for the ground of my obligation, I cannot find it in my obligation itself. But I believe it is possible to distinguish between the sense of duty in general, and that of a duty to realize a goodness connected with the particular principle of the action which is recognized as my duty now, though I may have no desire to do the action which this principle requires. The defence of this view will involve us in a discussion of the notion of good, which I believe to be more fundamental than that of right. This must be deferred for the present. Meanwhile, I wish to direct attention to the difference between motives like affection, or gratitude, and motives like the sense of the rightness of some particular principle of action, to the action required by which, in the actual situation, a man may have no such inclination as he may towards doing a particular kindness.

(3) At this point I may be charged with evading one objection by exposing myself to another more serious. The last objection was, that it cannot be my duty to act from a motive which I do not feel, and I cannot feel a motive to

order. It is no answer to this, it may be said, to say that it may be your duty to act from such motives as kindliness or gratitude when you do feel them; nor have you contended in reply that it is your duty to feel them. Instead, you have contended that when you do not feel any of them, it may be your duty to act from the sense of a particular duty. Is not this to make the rightness of the act which you ought to do, which rightness, you say, is the ground of your obligation to do it, consist in its being the act which you ought to do? And is not this to give away your whole case?

I would suggest in reply that there is a certain difference between the sense of obligation and such motives as kindliness, gratitude, affection, of which we must take account here. If a man does not feel gratitude or affection towards a particular person, he cannot summon it at will, nor can he summon at will a general benevolence. But if he is conscious of obligation, it is because the sense of an obligation to do some particular action is already there. It cannot be his duty to act from a sense of obligation, when he feels none. A man unconscious of obligation is not a moral subject; no character in whatever he might do could be a ground why he ought to do it, since he could have no duties; he might recognize goodness in the action, but it could not appear to him as rightness[1]; and if he is really unconscious of the obligation to do a particular act, say to pay his debts, he is not under obligation to pay them. If we think his present unconsciousness of this obligation to be due to his past failure to discharge obligations of which he was conscious, we do not hold him now excused. And perhaps, even without this, his present unconsciousness may be held evil in him.

[1] Cf. Kant, Preface to *Metaphysische Anfangsgründe der Tugendlehre*, p. 247; Hartenstein, vii. 203 (*E. T.*, T. K. Abbott's *Kant's Theory of Ethics*, p. 310), quoted, *infra*, p. 131.

But I have to distinguish between the consciousness of duty in general, and that of my duty to act in a particular way here and now. It is this latter that may be the motive making the rightness of the action which, when moved by the former to ask myself what I ought to do, I recognize as the ground why one act rather than another is my duty now: this latter which, in such a case, takes the place of a particular good motive like affection.

No one owes [1] to do anything, except in virtue of what he is, and what others are, and the situation in which he and they are placed; and if he is to be conscious of some particular obligation, he must be conscious, however in-explicitly, of all that. The primary and direct consciousness of obligation comes through consciousness of all that; i.e. it is consciousness of a determinate obligation to do this in this situation. A man may come to think of his particular obligations as each an instance of something particularizable in other ways than in this instance it is particularized; but that is secondary. Provided that he is conscious of the facts determining a present obligation to a particular action, the thought of himself acting thus in this situation may work with a sort of urgency in him to the doing of the act, even without his saying to himself that he ought to do it: still more, without his saying to him-

[1] I venture to write 'owes', and not 'ought', here and in some other places, because the past tense of 'ought' makes it apt to suggest what passes in the mind of a man judging the completed actions of himself or another. Now the consciousness of obligation seems to determine action otherwise than it determines judgement upon an action performed, although it is hard to state this difference in a satisfactory way. But this much may be said, that, whereas in determining action it may work without being reflected on, in determining judgement upon action performed, it must be reflected upon. The difference, whether that be the proper account of it or not, may, I think, be indicated where necessary by a distinction between 'owes' and 'ought'.

self that he ought to do this now, because duty (as something universal) requires it. What I have called the urgency of this thought is a motive, as a grateful or affectionate impulse is. A man in whom there is that urgency, and also some contrary inclination, if he asks how he ought to act and does what he thinks he ought to do, does it because he thinks it right; but what he thinks right is so because in it that urgency is preferred to or prevails over the contrary inclination, as a kindly impulse may be preferred to or prevail over one of self-indulgence: although that urgency differs from either of these, in its particular nature, as they do not differ from one another in theirs. For we recognize it as something not necessarily stronger than, but superior to, *any* particular desire we may feel at the same time; this is what Butler meant by the 'authority' as distinct from the 'power' of conscience. And if a man, feeling that urgency in a particular situation and some conflicting impulse as well, hesitates before acting, but recognizing this superiority acts as he now reflectively thinks he ought, it may be said without tautology that he then becomes conscious that he ought to act from a sense of obligation. I have still to show that there is a goodness in the act, the particular urgency in the thought of which makes the act done from a sense of it an act done from a sense of obligation.

Let me offer an example. Suppose that I have promised to take Paul to see a race, though I am not fond of Paul or his company, and that before the day of the race a friend of mine, Peter, whom I have not seen for many years, writes to ask me to meet him at the hour of the race elsewhere. Let us agree that, nevertheless, I ought to take Paul as promised. But I decide to break my promise; and then, at the last moment, Peter wires to me to meet him at the race instead. If now, after deciding to break my promise to Paul for the sake of meeting Peter, I take him because I am going anyhow, and not because I had promised to, I submit that I no more do a right than a moral act. For my duty is to take him because I had promised to, whereas I actually take him because I want to meet Peter. It is true that I could go to the race alone; and so far as, now that I am anyhow going, and in spite of my dislike of his company, because I promised I take him, there is something right about my action. I do not do what I ought, but I come nearer doing what I ought than if I had left him behind; as a man who owes another £100, and pays him £50 because he knows he ought to pay him £100, comes nearer to doing what he ought than if he had paid him nothing at all. These are, perhaps, examples of action from mixed motives. The motive which makes me go to the race is the desire to meet Peter; the motive which makes me, as I am going, take Paul is the obligation of the consciousness of my promise. But still I have not done what I ought. That was, to take Paul because I had promised to; whereas I do take him because I can keep my promise consistently with meeting Peter.

My obligation to take Paul originates in a situation in which I and he and the relations between us, consisting in my having promised to take him and his desiring me to fulfil my promise, all belong. But there must be consciousness in me of all this, if I am to be obliged. The person who ought to take him is I, but also is the person who promised. If then I am to be conscious of what I ought to do, or of the act right for me in this actual situation, I must be conscious of the promise and of its being mine. It would be an obviously incomplete account to say that I was aware of the obligation, but not aware that it was mine. It is equally incomplete to say that I am aware of my obligation to take him, but not of my obligation to take him because I promised. So far as I take him for any other reason, as because I am anyhow going, or because I fear that if I do not take him he will do me some ill turn, I do not do what I ought, what is right.

Aristotle made a distinction between doing what one ought, ἃ δεῖ, and doing as one ought, ὡς δεῖ. No doubt this was at bottom the same distinction as that between the moral act and the possibly valueless right act. But if I take Paul not because I promised, I neither do ἃ δεῖ nor ὡς δεῖ. It might be said that I do what I ought, ἃ δεῖ, if I take him because I promised, and as I ought, ὡς δεῖ, if I at the same time recognize the fulfilment of promises generally as a duty. But the other sense of the distinction seems to me mistaken, whether in Greek or English. Aristotle, where he expounds it [1], is contrasting art and conduct, τέχνη and πρᾶξις. But it is precisely because some works of art have a being beyond the making of them, whereas an act has no being outside the doing of it, that the contrast to which Aristotle draws attention arises. You can distinguish art from its products, τέχνη from τὰ ὑπὸ τῶν τεχνῶν γινόμενα. You cannot distinguish conduct from the actions in which it issues, σπουδαία πρᾶξις from τὰ κατὰ τὰς ἀρετὰς γινόμενα. Of products of art, therefore, it might be said that they have a goodness in them, τὸ εὖ ἔχει ἐν αὐτοῖς, though they came about of good fortune rather than artistic sense. That cannot be said of actions, if they come about of no good motive; they have then no rightness.

It is important to see that a man may act rightly, because moved by the thought, his being moved by which makes his act right, whether he thinks how he ought to act or not. The expression 'to be moved' is not adequate, because it suggests that the person is acted on, rather than acting. A man is in the thought or the desire that moves him, as

[1] *Eth. Nic.* II. iv.

much as they in him. The thought that he has promised obliges him by working in him, not as a body acts upon another body, but as the conception of some course or principle of action as good acts in a man to control inclination; this is the rule of the λογιστικόν, the rational, in the soul, to use Plato's language, which is not comparable to the rule of one man over another who does not give willing service. But if a man thinks of the relation which this thought, that he has promised, has or might have to his conflicting inclination, in making him fulfil his promise in spite of his inclination, as a particular instance of the relation of obliging thought to contrary inclination, and recognizes the common goodness belonging to such actions, then he acts from a sense of obligation.

I have been trying to describe what occurs in another man acting rightly without reflection, or reflectively from a sense of obligation. But he does not in acting realize his action to be such as I have described it. *Mutato nomine de me Fabula narratur*. When I am engaged in considering how I ought to act, and in acting, I am not also knowing exactly what is happening in me; that I can only do in retrospect, or in another. Therefore, when I imagine myself engaged in considering how I ought to act, and try to describe the 'right act' as it then presents itself to me, I am apt to misdescribe it as something into which the thought that moves me does not enter. But they are really a unity, like thought and its expression in speculative thinking.

(4) I have said that acting rightly is being moved by the thought, being moved by which makes the act right, to do the action; and that being moved by this thought is being obliged. (The consciousness of this relation, which is not that of one thing forcing another, is the consciousness of obligation.) But to this the objection may be, and has been,[1]

[1] By Professor H. A. Prichard, in a letter.

raised that 'to act, i.e. to do some particular action, rightly cannot *be* to be obliged by a certain thought to do a certain action'. For if to do a particular, or a certain, action *is* that, then to act is to be obliged by a certain thought to be obliged by a certain thought to be obliged . . . and so on without end.

The appearance of this vicious regress arises, I think, from the fact that action is self-realizing. Is it not true that an action is the realization or working out of an intended action? An intention does not lead to an action as the discharge of David's sling-stone led to the death of Goliath. But might not the same reduction be applied to this statement? An action is the realization or working out of an intended realization or working out of an intended. . . .? The answer is that in any self-realizing process, that which is ultimately realized is somehow involved in the determination of the process by which or in which it is realized. Physical science, no doubt, in treating its problems does not recognize the possibility of this.

When an artist designs, the thought of what is to be designed is at work, however inexplicitly, in completing the design. Until it is complete, he has not done what he is doing. To design, therefore, is to be determined by a certain thought to design. 'To be determined' is not to be acted on from without. The activity is spontaneous, but determinate. Its completion need not require that the artist should make anything which others can perceive: a drawing on paper, a volume of musical sound or a score, a written poem. He may do the whole 'in his head'. But he may be unable to do it 'in his head' except in the process of making something, and even if he is able, imagining must take the place of making.

In action there is not this kind of break allowed between thought and execution. It is the thought of *effecting* some new state of affairs that moves in me to realization, not the mere thought of a new state of affairs: this would be day-dreaming. An exception must be made for cases where what I resolve to do is to refrain from effecting any change. I may think, for example, that I ought not to become a candidate for some post which a friend is seeking; and if I have promised not to stand, and am tempted sorely nevertheless to stand, in doing right I am moved by the thought of holding back because I promised to hold back. Even here, there may be real inhibitions of physical impulses to be effected.[1]

What the artistic experience may be, that expresses itself 'outwardly' in what the artist makes for others to see or hear, cannot be known to them as it is to himself; and different 'inner' activities may pass into what would seem to observers the same execution. The most sympathetic observers would be best able to distinguish by nuances in the execution the precise nature of the working of the artist's mind. Somewhat similarly the 'outward action' may fail to betray all, the thought of which in the agent's mind moves him to what so displays itself. Yet some difference in what I do may be visible to a close observer, when I am moved to take Paul to see a race by the thought of my promise to take him, and when by the thought of

---

[1] Mr. E. F. Carritt has suggested to me that it is more correct to regard action as realizing itself not in bringing about a change, but in trying to bring about a change in some situation. This would bring action and refraining from action into closer accord. And no doubt to try is all that is in our power. There may always be physical obstacles to the execution of what we try to do. But it is only so far as we succeed in doing what we try to do, that one trying can be discriminated from another. And even trying has, I suppose, some physical expression, though it be one which is not ascertainable, in 'the interior beginnings of voluntary motion', to use Hobbes's phrase.

thus escaping an ill turn at his hands; or again, there may be differences of a physical kind, not discoverable, in which the act of refraining is expressed, when I am moved to abstain from standing for a post by the thought of thereby serving a friend at the sacrifice of my own inclination, and when by my dislike of certain incidents in the work involved. It may be added that just as there are artists (perhaps they are the majority) who only become fully aware of what they mean or are designing in executing their design so that others may see or hear, so men's purposes seem often unable to shape themselves except in action. And perhaps this may partly justify our tendency not to treat the resolution to commit a crime or do some noble act as equal, for a judgement on a man's character, to the commission of the crime or the performance of the noble action.

Only the thought of a *particular* action can be thus self-realizing, not that, e.g., of doing one's duty in general. And I think that when a man is moved by the thought of a particular action, as of keeping this promise, though there be no *inclination* to do for its own sake what he has promised to do, there need be no feeling of obligation. Honest men do not pay their debts because they feel obliged to, nor yet from an inclination to give money to the gentlemen who are their creditors. But if any contrary inclination should be stirred, then a man would begin to feel the obligatoriness of that, the thought of which was moving him. 'Feeling obliged', before action, is an emotional experience arising through the urgency of the thought of that which I feel obliged to do in the face of some inclination to act otherwise. Kant was, I think, correct in saying that a being whose will was 'holy' would not feel obliged. Perhaps he might understand, nevertheless, what obligation was. This urgency of what we feel obliged to do connects with a consciousness that it is better to act thus at the sacrifice of inclination, than vice versa. Therefore, when a man acts from a sense of obligation, he is not the theatre of a conflict between two particular desires; for where the thought that one course is better than another is at work, inclinations to two courses are not as it were fighting it out between themselves, and an interest in what is better is not a third particular interest.[1]

There is a further point. Not only, it seems to me, may I do my duty without a sense of obligation, and yet not from inclination to what is now in fact my duty for its own sake apart from its being my duty. I may also do it with a sense of obligation, but without the thought of or desire to do my duty in general. But if the consciousness that this particular action is my duty now moves me, or arouses a desire in me, to do this now, naturally the consciousness that something was my duty at another time would work similarly. It is, therefore, by a natural development that I pass from consciousness of particular obligations as occasions arise to the thought of duty as a general principle of action. But Kant failed in the attempt to show that from this I could pass, in the reverse direction, to a consciousness of my particular obligations. And so far as the determination of one's duty into its particulars is concerned, though there is no rule or criterion to be had, I think the notion of good is more helpful than that of right. This opinion is, of course, connected with what I have been already contending for, that my obligation to do what is right is to the performance not of an act without value, but of one which, if not related causally to good, must be somehow so related or in some way good itself.

[1] Cf. *supra*, pp. 22–4.

VI

AN AMBIGUITY IN THE WORD *RIGHT*

THE conviction that my obligation to do a particular action may be unconnected with any goodness in the act which I ought to do is perhaps connected with an ambiguity in the term 'right'.

It is not denied by those who hold this conviction that there is a ground of every obligation; but it lies in the particular character of the right act; I ought to keep a promise *because* I have promised, not *because* keeping a promise is right. Now we do often mean by calling an act right, that we ought to do it; and if we mean this, its rightness cannot be the *ground* of our obligation; it *is* our obligation. But do we not also use the word to mean some character in the act, because of which we ought to do it? If, as I think, we do, this character must be a sort of goodness. The difficulty here is to show what common form of goodness belongs to all right acts. For moral acts, we could state what this is, viz. that they are done from a sense of duty; but this cannot be the rightness in virtue of which it is our duty to do the acts. The difficulty, however, of finding a common goodness in all particular goods exists anyhow; it is at most aggravated by the admission of a subordinate community of goodness in the particular goods called right actions. To this problem I shall turn later.

A right act then may mean either an act which I ought to do, or an act having a rightness (a sort of goodness) in virtue of which I ought to do it. At least I take as some evidence that there is this equivocation in the word, and that it may escape notice, what seems to me an inconclusive argument developed by so careful a thinker as Professor

H. A. Prichard in his lecture on *Duty and Interest*. He there maintains that the proper English equivalent of δίκαιον in the *Republic* of Plato is 'right'. 'If we were to ask ourselves', he says [1], ' "What are Plato's words for right and wrong?" . . . we should have to allow' that they 'are not to be found in such words as χρῆ or δεῖ and their contraries, as in χρῆ δίκαιον εἶναι or ὅντινα τρόπον χρῆ ζῆν, where the subject is implied by the context to be τὸν μέλλοντα μακάριον ἔσεσθαι, but in δίκαιον and ἄδικον themselves. When he says of an action that it is δίκαιον, that is his way of saying that it is right, or a duty, or an act which we are morally bound to do. When he says that it is ἄδικον, that is to say that it is wrong. And in the sense in which we use the terms "justice" and "injustice", it is less accurate to describe what Plato is discussing as justice and injustice than as right and wrong. Our previous statement therefore' —i.e. the statement that the *Republic* is an elaborate attempt to show that, in spite of appearance to the contrary, it is by acting justly that we shall really gain, or become happy—'might be put in the form that Plato is mainly occupied in the *Republic* with attempting to shew it is by doing our duty, or what we are morally bound to do, that we shall become happy.'

There is plausibility in this. It is, I think, in a sense, less accurate to describe what Plato is discussing as justice and injustice than as right and wrong; but not for the reason given. The reason is that there are a wider and a narrower sense of δικαιοσύνη or ἀδικία, justice or injustice, which Aristotle marks by opposing ὅλη δικαιοσύνη to ἡ κατὰ μέρος δικαιοσύνη, complete to particular justice; and just acts in the narrow sense are only some of those just in the wider. But the reason given is that δικαιοσύνη means simply doing what you are morally bound to do. Now

[1] Loc. cit., p. 5.

no doubt the practice of ὅλη δικαιοσύνη, complete justice, is doing what you ought to do; but that is because what you ought to do is the acts springing from ὅλη δικαιοσύνη, not because saying that they spring from ὅλη δικαιοσύνη, or are in the wider sense δίκαια, means that you ought to do them.

It is clear that Plato did not mean by δίκαιον, as Aristotle preferred to, that particular character because of which we call an act just but not generous, nor courageous, nor friendly. If in English the word 'just' more naturally suggests the narrower meaning in which Aristotle preferred to use δίκαιον, then 'right' may be a better equivalent for δίκαιον as Plato uses it; but even so, it will be used of a character in all actions which we ought to do, as δίκαιον is used by Aristotle of a character in some of them. I do not know that 'right' and 'wrong' so readily suggest generic characters in actions, in virtue of which we ought to do or forbear them, as 'just' and 'unjust' suggest specific characters; maybe 'right' is more apt to suggest a character in virtue of which an act should be done, than 'wrong' one in virtue of which it should be forborne. But only if they do suggest generic characters can they render δίκαιον and ἄδικον, in Plato's sense, as 'just' and 'unjust' will render them in Aristotle's. For the difference in their use of the words is, I think, that between a wider and narrower extension; Plato means something which what Aristotle means has in common with acts that are generous, courageous, friendly, but not (in his sense) just. Now to be obligatory is not anything of this sort. Obligatoriness is not a character of actions. There is no ought-to-be-done-ness, or ought-to-be-forborne-ness. To say that an act is obligatory means that the doing it is obligatory on me. An obligatory act is like a well-remembered face; the face no doubt has characters because of which it is well remembered, but it is called well-remembered to signify not those characters, but that others remember it well. And an act is called obligatory because of some character which it has, but to signify not that character, but that we ought to do it because thereof.

Therefore, the statement that δίκαιον, in the *Republic*, means 'right' is defensible, so far as a 'right action', like a 'just action', may mean one of a character in virtue of which we ought to do it, and mean this with a greater range of variability indicated in the character than 'just' commonly indicates. But if the intention of the statement is that, by calling an act δίκαιον, Plato merely meant that we ought to do it, then I think it is incorrect. Now the argument to which I have referred as inconclusive is only inconclusive so long as 'right' or δίκαιον is taken in the sense expressly given to it by Professor Prichard, viz. that the act is one which we ought to do. If it can signify a character in virtue of which we ought, or it is alleged that we ought to do the action, the argument is sound. I take this fact as evidence that the word does also bear the second meaning; for unless he had so understood it, though without noticing the shift, I do not think he could have used the argument.

According to Professor Prichard, the refutation which Plato makes Socrates offer of the sophistic doctrine about justice in the *Republic* is not the proper refutation. The Sophists argued that the actions which men think to be duties are not really so, because they do not inure to the advantage of the agent; and they offered 'an account of how they and others came to make the mistake of thinking these actions just, i.e. right'.[1] Socrates tries to refute them

[1] *Duty and Interest*, p. 7. It is clear that by 'thinking these actions right' Professor Prichard here means precisely the same as by 'thinking them to be duties'. Another quotation will confirm

by showing that the actions in question *are* to the advantage of the agent; but that would do nothing to show them to be duties. What Plato should have made Socrates answer is that its not inuring to the advantage of the agent is wholly irrelevant to an act being his duty; and, therefore, by showing them not so to inure (if they could show it) the Sophists could not prove them not to be duties.[1]

Neither Socrates nor Plato would have admitted that it was irrelevant to the question whether an act was a man's duty, that it should inure to his advantage. Herein Professor Prichard holds them in error, and with that I am not at the moment concerned. What I wish to submit is that the Sophists, according to the *Republic*, did *not* offer an account of how 'they and others came to make the mistake of thinking those actions just which were not so', but they did say that it was a mistake to think them duties, so that to be just, or δίκαιον, and to be a duty cannot in the *Republic* have meant the same. I do not see that the Sophists offered an account of the origin of the mistake of thinking them duties.

According to the Sophists, δίκαιον *means* 'inuring to the advantage of another than the agent'.[2] Now they certainly did not argue that actions thought to inure to the advantage of another than the agent did not really do so. On the contrary, they argued that, exactly because they really did so,

this. 'There is really no need to consider in detail whether these arguments, ['designed to prove that *doing what is right* will be for the good of the agent'] 'are successful; for even if they are successful, they will do nothing to prove what they are intended to prove, viz. that the moral convictions of our ordinary life are true. Further, the attempts arise simply out of a presupposition which on reflection anyone is bound to abandon, viz. that conduciveness to personal advantage is what *renders an action a duty.*' (p. 16: italics mine.)   ' Ib., p. 16.

[2] *Rep.* i. 338 c. To the definition in ii. 359 A my argument would apply *mutatis mutandis*.

a man who was sufficiently powerful would not do them, and would flout any pressure put on him to do them. On the other hand they did hold that men made a mistake in thinking just actions were duties. Consequently they saw no reason why a powerful man should do them. Plato makes Thrasymachus express the view that it is a mistake by saying that it is folly to do them. In effect, Thrasymachus rejects the notion of duty. No one, according to the sophistic position, really believes in this thing called duty. In that case no one can really make the mistake of thinking that anything is a duty. The only mistake he could make would be, to think it wise to do the actions called by the name.

That is why I do not see how the Sophists offered an account of the origin of the mistake of thinking just actions to be duties. This point is parenthetical to my main argument, but it is of sufficient interest to justify a parenthesis. It is really very difficult to see how on their theory words like duty have come into being. They, and many since who have taken up the same position, failed altogether to see the difficulty; and, therefore, they failed to offer a solution of it. The solution would have to consist, not in accounting for the mistake of thinking certain actions to be duties in the sense which their opponents allege the word to bear, because they say there is no such sense; but in accounting for men coming to use the word as if they meant something by it when they meant nothing. The same problem arises about the existence of other terms by which it is said that men are so mistaken as to think they mean something when there is nothing to mean. *Necessity* is an example. One method of solution is to say that the word stands for a peculiar feeling; thus to say that an act is a duty means that I have a peculiar feeling in thinking of it. Whether he does mean this a man can only ask, and answer, for himself. But we must return from this digression.

The Sophists, then, it may be allowed, held that men had made the mistake of thinking that just actions were duties, or that men ought to do what is just. This was not because they held there was something else that men ought to do (though they held there was something else which wise men would do); for in the vulgar sense of the word they said there were no duties. The reason why men were mistaken in thinking that they ought to do just actions was that it did not really pay them. Socrates ought, according to Professor Prichard, to have replied that that has nothing to do with it; instead, he tried to show that to do just actions does pay them. Now if the word 'just' here, which is the equivalent of the Greek δίκαιον, means some character in actions which can be thought the ground of a duty to do them, this argument is perfectly fair. Though one may dissent from the doctrine that it is irrelevant to the question whether an act is my duty that it should pay me (λυσιτελεῖν) in every possible sense of that word, that is another issue. But Professor Prichard says that δίκαιον in the *Republic*, which in this argument is rendered by 'just', really means 'right'; and by calling an action right he thinks he means merely that it is my duty. If that is so, when the Sophists said that men made the mistake of thinking that just actions were duties, they meant that men made the mistake of thinking that duties were duties. They cannot have meant that. And so only if 'right', as the equivalent of δίκαιον, means something else than being one's duty, will the argument stand. All Professor Prichard's statements will be found to be plausible, or have a good sense, in their context; and this could not be, but for a shift in the sense of 'right' from context to context. In one sense, it means that one ought to do the action so called; in the other, that it has a character for the sake of which one ought to do it. In this sense, it is the equivalent of Plato's δίκαιον; and when δίκαιον bears this sense, one *can* ask whether it is a mistake to think that what is δίκαιον is right in the other sense.

When the Sophists asked themselves what was the common character of the so-called just (or right) actions which men mistakenly thought obligatory (or, in the other sense, right), they said that it was their inuring to the advantage of another than the agent. That is not the whole account of what they thought about them; they thought such actions were also done reluctantly, or, as we say, under compulsion; though strictly a man is not compelled to do an action harmful to himself which he does for fear of worse evil from omitting it. This, however, was in their view the only real meaning of an action's obligatoriness. In this sense of 'oblige', a man may be obliged to do what is not in itself to his own advantage. In the ordinary sense, which, though they held that in it the word was a *vox nihili*, they imputed to unenlightened minds, they denied that just actions, i.e. actions inuring to the advantage of another than the agent, were obligatory. On their interpretation of 'just', that is an answer to a perfectly proper question, though it may be the wrong answer. But if 'just', i.e. δίκαιον, *meant* obligatory, it would be a silly question to ask whether just actions were obligatory.

But a question which is proper when 'just', or (as Professor Prichard prefers to render δίκαιον) 'right', means inuring to the advantage of another than the agent, remains proper on any other interpretation which makes it stand for a character of the actions about which it is asked whether they are obligatory. It ceases to be proper only if the word means being obligatory. One of the lessons of the *Republic*, however, is the great difficulty of finding a common character in all δίκαια, all just or right actions, that can be the reason why we ought to do them. The palpable nature (if one may so abuse that word) of inuring to the advantage of another and not the agent, makes that, to any one looking for an identical rightness in all right actions, seem the sort of answer he wants. In Plato's view, or in Socrates', no answer can be truly given which offers such a palpable identity; and as these various actions are still called δίκαια, or right, it is easy, when we have rejected any palpable identity of rightness as the *ground* of obligation, to slip into thinking that the identity meant *is* the common obligatoriness.

We are thus brought to the problem whether in the actions which we ought, or think we ought, to do there is any common character for the sake of which we ought, or think we ought, to do them. And perhaps we may be allowed to assume that, if there be, inuring to the advantage of another than the agent is not it. Now this is not an easy problem. Its difficulty, as I have said [1], is that of the unity of good. Plato, when he wrote the *Republic*, thought there somehow was such a character. Professor Moore thinks so, when he writes that an action is a duty because it will produce most good, good being a 'simple, indefinable, unanalysable object of thought'.[2] So do the Utilitarians, when they say that we ought to do on any occasion what will produce more pleasure and less pain than any alternative action then in our power. If they are all wrong, and there is no such character, our obligations will be an unconnected heap. That conclusion is disconcerting to philosophy, which attempts to bring a diversity of facts under some unity of principle. And we might be tempted to say that if there is no one reason for the one fact about all these various actions, that we ought to do them, there

[1] *Supra*, p. 59.   [2] *Principia Ethica*, § 15, p. 21.

is no reason. And then the conviction that we ought to do them might be in danger of seeming irrational.

Professor Prichard allows that the judgement that I ought to do some *particular* action would be irrational, if no reason could be given why I ought to do *that* action. 'Wherever', he says, 'in ordinary life we think of some particular action as a duty, we are not simply thinking of it as right, but also thinking of its rightness as constituted by the possession of some definite characteristic other than that of being advantageous to the agent. For we think of the action as a particular action *of a certain kind*, the nature of which is indicated by general words contained in the phrase by which we refer to the action, e.g. "*fulfilling* the *promise* which we made to X yesterday", or "*looking after* our *parents*". And we do not think of the action as right *blindly*, i.e. irrespectively of the special character which we think the act to possess; rather we think of it as being right in virtue of possessing a particular characteristic of the kind indicated by the phrase by which we refer to it.' [1] And because these and other such definite characteristics cannot be generalized as instances of conducing to the agent's advantage, he adds that 'if we were to maintain that conduciveness to the agent's advantage is what renders an action right, we should have to allow that any of our ordinary moral convictions, so far from being capable of vindication, is simply a mistake, as being really the conviction that some particular action is rendered a duty by its possession of some character which is not that of being advantageous.' [2]

But that the characteristics which render particular actions duties cannot be generalized as instances of conducing to the agent's advantage does not show that they can be brought under no generalization consistently with

[1] *Duty and Interest*, pp. 15, 16.   [2] Ib., p. 16.

our ordinary moral convictions. Any generalization which could not, as (in my opinion) those of Professor Moore and the Utilitarians can, be shown to be false is bound, I think, at first to seem unsatisfactory: though, perhaps, on further reflection it might begin to commend itself. But at any rate the question is one which can be raised, even if we should in the end conclude that no such generalization is possible. Professor Prichard, however, seems to think that it cannot be raised.

Plato asks the question 'What is justice?'. Professor Prichard gives three alternative amplifications of this question: 'What is the characteristic the possession of which by an action necessitates that the action is just, i.e. an action which it is our duty, or which we ought, to do?': 'What renders a just or right action, just or right?': 'What is the characteristic common to particular just acts which renders them just?' [1]. Having given them, he proceeds as follows: 'For any one even to ask this question is to imply that he already *knows* what particular actions are just. For even to ask "What is the character common to certain things?" is to imply that we already *know* what the things are of which we are wanting to find the common character. Equally, of course, any attempt to answer the question has the same implication. For such an attempt can only consist in considering the particular actions which we know to be just and attempting to discover what is the characteristic common to them all, the vague apprehension of

[1] Ib., p. 17. It will be noticed that here again 'just' or 'right' is used in two senses. 'What is justice?' means 'What is the *characteristic which*, &c.' Here justice or rightness is the ground of something else. But that which it is the ground of in an action possessing it is its being 'just, that is an act which it is our duty, or which we ought, to do.' Here justice or rightness is that of which before it was the ground, viz. that we ought to do the action.

which has led us to apprehend them to be just. Plato, therefore, both in representing Socrates as raising with his hearers the question "What is justice?" and also in representing them all as attempting to answer it, is implying, whether he is aware that he is doing so or not, that they all know what particular acts are, and what particular acts are not just.' And he goes on to argue that if the members of the dialogue had not *known* that certain [1] acts are just, they could only have been inquiring what they thought justice was, and not what it was really.

Here surely we have that 'short way with dissenters' invented by Gorgias, and dealt with by Socrates in the *Meno* and by Aristotle in the *Posterior Analytics* [2]; a man can learn either nothing or what he knows already. Granted that I cannot know there is such a thing as justice sufficiently to ask what it is, without having identified it in *some* actions which I therefore know to be just: it does not follow that I have identified it in *all* particular actions which are just, or could recognize it in others until I have clarified my thought of what it is in those which I do know to be just. For there are characters, I suppose (as indeed Aristotle says in the passage referred to [3]), which we may at once know and not know; we may know them enough to search into their nature further. Goodness, beauty, truth, perhaps rightness, are such characters. It can hardly be maintained that no one can ask the question 'What is truth?' without implying that he already knows what

[1] 'Certain acts' here should, in consistency with the language used previously, include all the particular acts that are just.

[2] Plato, *Meno* 80 D, E; Aristotle, *Post. An.* I. i. 5, 71ᵃ 30 ἢ γὰρ οὐδὲν μαθήσεται ἢ ἃ οἶδεν.

[3] *Post. An.* I. i. 7 ἀλλ' οὐδὲν (οἶμαι) κωλύει, ὃ μανθάνει, ἔστιν ὡς ἐπίστασθαι, ἔστι δ' ὡς ἀγνοεῖν· ἄτοπον γὰρ οὐκ εἰ οἶδέ πως ὃ μανθάνει, ἀλλ' εἰ ὡδί, οἷον ᾗ μανθάνει καὶ ὥς.

particular judgements are true. Professor Prichard himself speaks of our *vague* apprehension of the characteristic
common to all just actions which has led us to apprehend
them to be just. But if we apprehend a character vaguely,
we shall know less where it lies. The vague apprehension
of a character is one which, while sufficing us to pick up
some subjects possessing it, leaves us liable to overlook it
in others, or to the mistake of thinking we have found it
where it is not. Surely in all search for definitions the
knowledge what subjects are of the kind to be defined and
the knowledge of the definition of the kind advance together; or, if the second cannot properly be said to advance,
since it is knowledge of what is one, whereas the first can,
being of many, in coming to know what is the definition
of the kind we at the same time advance in our knowledge
of what subjects belong to the kind.

Men, therefore, may at once know that certain actions
are just or right, and erroneously think that others are, not
less if their justice or rightness is a common characteristic
of such actions than if it is the fact that men ought to do
them. They may also know that there is such a character
as justice in actions, and know or think that it is their duty
to do the actions which have it, even before they know
what precisely that character is. For it is a character of
that peculiar sort, like truth, beauty, and goodness, that
we can seek it, as Plato says, 'divining it to be something' [1],
before we know what it is, and, therefore, also before we
know fully where it is. Whether the actions which men
ought to do—be it that they know or only think at present
that they ought to do them—have all in fact a common
rightness in virtue of which men ought to do them, is still
our question. But there is no ground for saying that we

[1] *Rep*. vi. 505 E ἀπομαντευομένη τι εἶναι. He is speaking of
good.

cannot ask the question 'What is justice?' or 'What is rightness?' as a character common to all actions which we ought to do, and because of or for the sake of which we ought to do them, without implying that we already know what acts are just or right, and therefore incumbent on us. If this were so, then, since there are sufficient disputes about what is right to prove that the condition on which would depend the possibility of asking the question is not fulfilled, we could not ask it. But since we can ask it, therefore, until we have the answer, it may even be an open issue, to a man who knows that there are actions which it is right, in the sense of being his duty, to do, whether just actions, or actions right in the other sense, of having the character which we have not yet precisely ascertained, are they. In any case, we may now turn to look for the common character—if there really is one—of all just or right actions, on account of which it is alleged that we ought to do them.

VII

RIGHT AND GOODNESS

WE have to consider whether there is any character common to right acts, in virtue of which it is that we think we ought to do them. If there is, this character may be named their rightness, or be what is meant when they are called δίκαια. Now the first point I wish to make is that, if there is such a character in right acts, it is not one that can properly be called a *quality* of them. It must, I think, be a form of goodness, if it is at all. Secondly, it will not help us to examine acts, the obligation to do which arises merely from their being means to some good.

Professor Moore agrees so far with the Utilitarians as to hold that rightness in actions is always being causally related to some good; the goodness is not intrinsic to a right action. He only differs from the Utilitarians about the nature of this intrinsic goodness. If the view that he and they share be correct, and right actions can be called good only as means, then at any rate their rightness is not a quality. If a stands in the relation R to b, even though R were the causal relation, it is not a quality of a. Some writers have supposed that there must be a relational property in a, of standing in the relation R to b, as well as the relation R in which a stands to b. Leibniz, who thought that every real or substance was independent of every other, except for the common dependence of all finite substances on God, denied that relations were real; they were mere ideal things, somewhat which appeared to us, or which we imagined to be, when the things said to stand in them were of certain sorts (for one must not say, when they had natures related in a certain way). Thus in strictness, according to him, we are to think that David's being the father of Solomon is two facts: 'aliud esse paternitatem in David, aliud filiationem in Salamone'. I do not think this doctrine will stand working out, though, if we reject it certain consequences follow, difficult no doubt as well regarding essence and personality, on which something will be said in the last chapter.

I hardly see, indeed, how the introduction of a relational property really helps us to understand the fact of one thing being in relation to another. To have the relational property seems to be only another form of words for standing in the relation. For by the relational property is not meant what is called the *fundamentum relationis*. If a dog is running faster than a man, it is primarily not the dog and the man, but the velocities of the dog and of the man, that are related; the dog and the man are related only through their velocities. These velocities are properties in them, and they are the *fundamenta relationis*. But the relational properties which I call in question would be properties of the dog's velocity and of the man's velocity, not of the dog and of the man: the properties in each velocity of standing in a certain relation to the other velocity; and I do not see what these are more than the relation. For the relational property in the dog's velocity of being faster than the man's, and in the man's of being slower than the dog's, would themselves differ and be related, and need further relational properties, concerning which the same difficulty would arise again, and so *ad infinitum*. The doctrine is a variant of Bradley's, when he argued that the relation of a to b belongs, and is therefore itself related, to a by a further relation[1]; and the relation of belonging to a, which connects with a its relation to b, must again be related to a by another relation; and so *ad infinitum*. From which it will be remembered that Bradley concludes that the

[1] F. H. Bradley, *Appearance and Reality*, ch. iii.

relational form, under which the one real appears to us as a multiplicity of related reals, belongs only to appearance, and is lost in the absolute. But perhaps we should reply with Cook Wilson that the business of a relation is to relate; and then, whether we think or not that the relational form disappears in the absolute, we may drop relational properties and relations which relate relations to their terms. Even, however, if there be relational properties, they will not be qualities; there is a fundamental distinction between ποιόν and πρός τι, between being a velocity and its being greater than another.

What we may call the instrumental view of the nature of rightness, then,—that what is right is instrumental to the being of what is intrinsically good—does not make of rightness a common quality in all that is right. Equally is this true if right is intrinsic goodness of some sort, supposing that goodness is not a quality; and so we may for the moment leave it undecided whether there is any right act whose rightness is an intrinsic goodness, to defend the assertion that goodness is not a quality. If that can be established, rightness, which is either a form of goodness or instrumental to some good, will not be a quality.

That goodness is not a quality is the burden of Aristotle's argument in the *Nicomachean Ethics*, I. vi, though equally the teaching of Plato in the *Republic*. The failure to appreciate, or at least to express himself as if he appreciated this seems to me a weak point in what is otherwise one of the most valuable contentions in Professor Moore's *Principia Ethica*. Professor Moore takes good to be the fundamental notion of Ethics, and there I believe he is right, with the Greeks. 'That which is meant by "good" is,' he says, 'in fact, except its converse "bad", the *only* simple object of thought which is peculiar to Ethics', and the question how it is to be defined 'is the most fundamental question in all Ethics'.[1] We learn, however, in the next section that it is indefinable; but *the* good is not so: i.e. we may define those subjects which have goodness; what we cannot define is the goodness which they have. Indeed he says that if he did not think *the* good could be defined, he would not be writing on Ethics; though the word 'designated' seems to me more proper here than 'defined'. For the chief business of Ethics, he thinks, is to ascertain what subjects have this indefinable goodness or 'to decide the question "What things have intrinsic value and in what degrees?"'; the chief, in his opinion, being personal affections and aesthetic enjoyments.[2] But he only designates these as the chief, and does not attempt to define them, at least in what he says is the most important sense of the word 'define', viz. that 'in which a definition states what are the parts which invariably compose a certain whole'.[3] It is because, in his view, good or goodness 'is simple and has no parts' that it has no definition.[3] It is 'a simple and indefinable quality. There are many other instances of such qualities. Consider yellow, for example'.[4] Yellow, he very properly points out, is not the 'kind of light-vibrations' which 'must stimulate the normal eye, in order that we may perceive it'. To know what yellow is we must just see *it*. But far too many philosophers, he thinks, have made about good a mistake like that which people make about yellow when they say that yellow *is* light-vibrations of a certain kind; and far too many people, I allow, make it about yellow: more, perhaps, than really make it about good. But Professor Moore thinks that all philosophers, except Henry Sidgwick, who have contended that pleasure, or happiness, or self-realization, or acting on that principle which one can will to be law universal is

[1] Loc. cit., § 5, p. 5.   [2] Ib., §§ 112, 113, pp. 187, 189.
[3] Ib., § 10, p. 9.   [4] Ib., § 10, p. 10.

good, and alone good, have been guilty of the fallacy (which he names the Naturalistic fallacy) of identifying good or goodness with something else than itself; so that 'pleasure is good', or 'self-realization is good', and so forth, would have no more meaning, if true, than that the word 'good' stands for pleasure, or for self-realization (with which they erroneously identify good), not for something unique and distinct from what the word 'pleasure' or the word 'self-realization' stands for. But 'good' stands for something simple and unanalysable: for what has no other nature or being than a simple one, and so is unique. If, then, the subject-term, 'pleasure', 'self-realization', or what not, stands for anything, it must either stand for the same simple unanalysable nature as 'good' does, or for something else. On the first alternative, the proposition merely tells you that 'good' is a name for the same simple unanalysable nature for which 'pleasure' or 'self-realization' is a name. On the second, it identifies whatever 'pleasure' or 'self-realization' is the name of with something not that, of which 'good' is the name, and so is false.

All this, if I may say so, seems to me error. Professor Moore thinks that good is a quality, unanalysable in the same sort of way as yellow; and his only excuse, so far as I see, is that goodness is *one* character. But everything that can be defined is one; that does not make it false to identify the multiplicity recognized in the definition with the unity of what is defined. A definition, says Professor Moore, states what are the parts which invariably compose a certain whole. But the parts are not separates brought into aggregation; their whole is not a sum. His argument seems to suppose with Hume that whatever is distinguishable is separable, and to make no distinction between the relation to one another of the parts reached in a physical, and that of those reached in a metaphysical division (to use the language of the Schools). If anything is simple and unanalysable like yellow, it cannot be defined; but it does not follow that, if it can be defined, it is not one, though definition sets out a many. I allow that yellow is an excellent example of a simple quality; for that reason it is excellent to contrast with good, not to compare with it. The theology of the schoolmen seems to me to show a far better understanding of the matter than does the argument of Professor Moore. God, they said, is not to be called good, but goodness. Why? Because his goodness cannot be thought of as a quality, which he might get or lose, like the yellow of a Magnum Bonum plum, as it ripens and then decays. There is nothing in the being of God which does not contribute to, and indeed is not needed for, his goodness; he is good as a perfectly healthy body is healthy, through and through. But none the less goodness in him is one, as health is one; only it is not simple, any more than God or health is simple. After all, it may be thought that God is one, but not that he is simple and unanalysable. Rather, he is infinitely complex; and the reason why he—or for that matter any finite individual having the nature of a person—is indefinable is infinite complexity, not simplicity nor being one. How could you define what was not one? Two would require two definitions. What is peculiar about good is that, if you could define *the* good or what has goodness (which Professor Moore says can be defined), you would thereby define its good or goodness (which he says is indefinable). That holds for any subject which *is* good, i.e. which is not a 'somewhat else' wherein that which *is* good is lodged, ὡς ἐν ὑποκειμένῳ. It is true of the goodness of a poem, which is really identical with the poem, though not with the poet, in whom the poem as his work is lodged in the making. If the poet in turn is good, his goodness is identical with him, as this spiritual being, though not with the body in which this spiritual being is (on one view) supposed to be lodged. But in God it is not commonly thought that there is this conjunction of soul and body; he is said to be without body, parts, or passions; he is not lodged in something else. In him then more manifestly than elsewhere, both for this reason and because his goodness is perfect, this identity holds. He and his goodness are one; he is not good but goodness. So in the *Republic* the ἰδέα τοῦ ἀγαθοῦ is one with the ἀγαθόν whose form it is. All this the schoolmen understood, and it is a pity that it should be forgotten. For its truth is not dependent on the correctness of the theological form in which they stated it. If there is any completely real which is completely good, the doctrine holds of it; it is a metaphysical doctrine, not a theological. But a completely real is a substance, not a quality; it is about as unlike yellow as anything can be. And so is goodness, in any form it takes. Suppose there can be a perfectly good poem: one in which everything is good, or (as we may say) just right, so that to alter it in any way would be to make it less good. The more completely it is a unity, the nearer it comes to being perfectly good; for unity too is good. *Its* goodness could not be apprehended or learnt by reading a different poem, nor without reading this; and the only definition of its goodness is really the poem itself: which is also the only definition of the poem (so far as one may speak of defining the individual). And yet the more completely the poem is a unity, the less adequate to its nature is it to describe it as a whole of parts, though, of course, it is that as well; and the less adequate to the nature of its goodness is it to call it simple and unanalysable, though, of course, in a certain sense, that is true of it too; for its goodness is one, unitary, not an aggregation of different goodnesses, like that of *mens sana in corpore sano*, or of a well-furnished bran-pie. It cannot, if one may put it so, be broken up, though it can in a sense be analysed; we may call attention to factors or aspects of it. For what we may call analysis in problems like this is not what the chemist calls analysis in the laboratory, nor the mathematician when he considers a curve.

I conclude then that goodness is not a quality; and to be productive of good or goodness is not a quality. If, then, the character in virtue of which right actions are right is either being productive of good or goodness or an intrinsic goodness of some sort, it follows that there is no common *quality* in virtue of which right actions are right. A common quality would, no doubt, be much easier to recognize. On the other hand, when we found, as we soon should, that no common quality was leaping to sight, we might be less concerned if we could say to ourselves that after all that was not what we were looking for.

I confess to wondering what Professor Moore means when he speaks of a quality, or else what sort of experience he has when he thinks of or feels personal affections and aesthetic enjoyments and any elements of these which also are (as he allows) intrinsically good; though, as he adds, the degree of goodness in the wholes to which such elements belong is no direct function of and far exceeds that in any of the elements: a fact because of which he calls the wholes organic, but which is really intelligible, I think, only in the light of the considerations urged above, which he ignores. For he seems to think that he can find in all these, in the organic wholes and in these elements of them alike, an identical quality recognizable as yellow is recognizable in all yellow bodies. It would solve some difficulties for me if I could; but I certainly cannot.

Now Plato offered a definition of δικαιοσύνη, justice, which he thought held of every man or state, and every act of a man or state, that could be truly called δίκαιον. I need hardly quote it—τὸ τὰ αὑτοῦ πράττειν καὶ μὴ πολυπραγ-μονεῖν—to do one's own job and not interfere. But we must remind ourselves that a state or its acts are only just when its citizens do their own jobs; a man or his acts are only so when the different elements of his soul do theirs. That is, he recognized that justice is precisely of that sort of which we found goodness to be; it is one character, but it requires for its being the co-operation of 'parts' having their own different beings. However, the same may be said of health, of beauty, perhaps of truth, and these are not the characters which make just acts just. There are then divers characters of the sort in question. Might not just acts be made just, some by one character, some by another, so long as all these characters are of the sort in question?

The objection which suggests itself to such a view is that which Aristotle felt in regard to particular goods or ἀγαθά. The goodness of different particular goods is not the same, and yet one would think that some sort of identity must unite them, for them all to be called by the same name, good; οὐ γὰρ ἔοικε τοῖς γε ἀπὸ τύχης ὁμωνύμοις[1]—they do not seem like accidental homonyms. So with the rightness of right acts. It is perfectly correct to say, with Professor Prichard[2], that there is something in the nature of every right action on account of which we ought, or think we ought, to do it; for if not—if it were merely for its being an action, and not an action of some definite sort rather than another—it would be our duty to do anything that was an action, and life should be unbroken restlessness. 'Man hath still either toyes or care; He hath no root, nor to one place is ty'd, But ever restless and irregular About this earth doth run and ride.' But Vaughan offered that as a description of man's evil state, not of his virtue. Yet Professor Prichard's statement hardly seems a

---

[1] *Eth. Nic.* I. vi. 12, 1096ᵇ 26.　　　[2] *Vide* supra, p. 68.

sufficient account of why we say that certain acts are right, and ought to be done. For if we mean, as he says we do, by using the word 'right', no more than that we ought to do the action so called, it implies how the thought of a certain action moves a good man, but not what the character thought of in the action is. Now why should the thought of certain actions move a good man in what after all is the same way, viz. to the doing of them in despite of contrary inclination and to feeling a certain emotion withal, while the thought of other actions does not move him in this way, if there is nothing the same in the actions, the thought of which does so move him, distinguishing them from those, the thought of which does not? Obviously we cannot reply that the required identity is their being such that the thought of them so moves him. Either 'such that' means 'having a character because of which', and then the answer to the question 'What is the identical character?' is 'The identical character'; or else it is a mere periphrasis for being that of which the thought moves him, and we are offered, as the common character in actions in virtue of which the thought of them so moves a man, their being the actions of which the thought so moves him. That is like saying that what causes an effect is the causing it. At any rate there would then be no difficulty about 'plurality of causes'. As many heterogeneous agents as you like might cause indistinguishable changes in subjects of the same sort, since their causing the same effects would be itself the identical character in them which explained why, in spite of *their* being heterogeneous, their effects in things of the same sort were not. This will hardly do, in ethical or any other theory. No doubt it may be pointed out that conduct is not a field of the same causal relations as physical nature; but I do not think that matters here. Unless acting freely is acting without a reason, you need a reason of the same

sort for acting in the same way—for doing actions and not
forbearing them. I confess then that I am not content with
a set of mere different special natures in different right
actions, as equal but alternative grounds of my obligation
to do them. And there is evidence that this discontent has
been widely felt, in the efforts of Plato at once to define
δικαιοσύνη and to make all the actions of a good man's life
instances of it; in Aristotle's unwillingness to allow that
particular goods have that same name by mere accident;
in the various attempts of those who take the instrumental
view of rightness to bring under a common notion, of
pleasure or happiness or Professor Moore's simple indefinable, those results in their conduciveness to which the
instrumental rightness of right actions consists.

Yet I find no account of the common goodness of right
actions that altogether satisfies me. I will, however, put
forward four points for consideration, and three of them
at once: (1) Firstly, I think, as was said above, that the
rightness in a right action (when it is not instrumental) is a
sort of goodness; our problem, therefore, is that of the
unity of goodness in different goods. (2) Secondly, as we
have seen, it is not a common quality; and in the highest,
and in some examples of what is good, the goodness is at
once (a) identical with what is good, because nothing that
goes to constitute the being of what is good falls outside
of, or does not also go to constitute, its goodness; and also
(b) distinguishable from what is good, as a unitary or
single character is distinguishable from the diversity in
and because of which it is present. (3) Thirdly, I would
suggest that in very many things good of their kind this
peculiar relation, between a unitary goodness and a
diversity or multiplicity at once distinguishable from and
somehow identical with it, is plainly found. You may call
this a certain form of being in such things; and this, not

any quality, might turn out to be the common character of which we are in search. I say 'might'; but unfortunately there are, or seem to be, particular goods, instances of good, in which we cannot find this structure, or form of being. Some pleasures, sounds, colours, scents, perhaps even some emotions might be suggested; and some actions which we should call right, when we ask, before doing, what we ought to do, are at least very simple: as to answer truly an awkward question put to one.

There are those who would object that sounds and scents and colours cannot properly be enumerated with emotions and actions in a list of goods; nothing is really good except some form of spiritual activity. But I would not confine the term to forms of spiritual *activity*, unless 'activity' is to cover all actualized being of a spirit; in a world without mind and consciousness I do not think there would be good. And the colours I mean are colours delighting the heart, the sounds those that ravish the ear, the scents those that 'live within the sense they quicken'. If in the world of our experience we can pick out certain sounds and colours and scents without which life would be a poorer thing, I should say these are good.

They are good, however, only because they are elements in a life or experience which is good. Though I think Professor Moore is right in his account of the principle of 'organic wholes' when he says that the value of the whole 'need not be the same as the sum of the values of its parts', he appears to hold, and if so, I would urge, mistakenly, that the parts may have some value as mere parts. He takes the consciousness of a beautiful object. That 'is a thing of great intrinsic value; whereas the same object, if no one be conscious of it, has certainly comparatively little value, and is commonly held to have none at all'. He proceeds to distinguish, as the other element in the whole whose value is so great (viz. in the consciousness of a beautiful object), mere consciousness. This 'occurs as part of a different whole, whenever we are conscious of anything; and it would seem that some of these wholes have at all events very little value, and may even be indifferent, or positively bad. Yet we cannot always attribute the slightness of their value to any positive demerit in the object which differentiates them from the consciousness of beauty; the object itself may approach as near as possible to absolute neutrality.' Hence we cannot explain the little value in the whole, viz. in the consciousness of such object, by saying that the great positive demerit of the object factor has cancelled the high value of the factor consciousness, and we must hold that mere consciousness is not of high value. Neither is a beautiful object of which no one is conscious. Yet consciousness of a beautiful object has very high value. The high value of this whole, therefore, cannot be the sum of the values of its parts; for these are small.[1]

The principle of organic wholes seems to me here wrongly conceived. The wholes get their value from the natures of their parts, but they are not aggregates whose parts have values in isolation, but whose total values are not the sums of the values of their parts. It will be time to ask what is the value of *mere* consciousness, when mere consciousness has been shown to be something. If it is good to be conscious of a beautiful object, surely that is because the beautiful object is good; as Plato said that that thought is good which is of what is good.[2] But the relation of consciousness to its beautiful object is not like that of a beggar's fingers to some perfect jewel lying by the roadside, which he may pick up. We think of the being of the jewel as indifferent to there being any one to pick it up. The

---

[1] *Principia Ethica*, § 18, p. 28.   [2] *Rep.* vi. 505 c.

object of consciousness is not thus indifferent to conscious-ness. I would go so far on the way with those who hold that nothing is good except some form of spiritual activity, as to say that nothing is good except in a universe which includes, and is known to and therefore in a sense included in, mind. If we speak, as we do, of the perfection of some plant or animal or 'perfect work', it is because we seem to see in these the perfect realization of a plan or purpose; and a plan or purpose is a spiritual activity. If in a plant or animal it can work unconsciously, yet it comes to self-consciousness in some way at last. A world that could *never* come to self-consciousness, to realizing what it was both in the sense of actualizing it, and in that of being an object of consciousness to minds in which also it actualized itself, could have no goodness; but we may by anticipation call good some part whose nature is not yet in both senses realized; διὰ τὴν ἐλπίδα μακαρίζονται.[1]

However, the factors whose consideration has led us into this last discussion were not themselves of this sort, 'organic unities', such as organisms are. They were rather simples, some pleasures, sounds, scents, very uncomprehensive actions: in which it is difficult to find the peculiar form or structure that consists in being a manifold reduced to unity by the way in which the details conspire to constitute for the whole a goodness which is one. But the burden of the discussion was this, that the goodness which is an 'organic unity' is not the goodness of a whole whose elements, while having being and value in singleness and isolation, have not such values in isolation as will account for that of the whole. Rather, they are elements which, if not elements in this whole, are so in some other, and have no being nor value except in some whole.

(4) This brings me to the last of the four points which

---

[1] Aristotle, *Eth Nic.* I. ix. 10, 1100ᵃ 3.

I wish to put forward for consideration. Though we do not find those simple factors each good because in each we can discern that structure or form of being of which I spoke, yet neither do we find them good without looking beyond them, and seeing them as elements in some whole which has that structure. I believe that to be the thought at the bottom of Plato's doctrine, that even justice is not known to be good until it is seen as an element required for the good of the one all-including real, for the ἰδέα τοῦ ἀγαθοῦ which is the only true goodness, because it is the good of the intelligible reality that is not good but goodness.

VIII

THE RIGHTNESS OF RIGHT ACTIONS

BEFORE attempting to test the suggestion that such particulars as we find good, without being able to see their goodness as a unitary character constituted by the detailed nature of what is good, may be themselves detail in the nature of a more comprehensive system, whose goodness can be so viewed, I wish to meet a preliminary objection that might be made. It does not matter, it might be said, whether it is so or not; for it is of no importance, even if true, that good is a form of unity in what is good such as you have tried to describe. It is not the being unified in a certain way that matters, but what that is wherein this form of unity is found.

Certainly it is not one without the other. But we may remember Kant's doctrine of the good will. It is one which wills under the conception of a rule determining the multiplicity of all action to which it might apply into accordance with itself. It has often been objected that Kant's good will is purely formal, and that to 'realize self-consistency' is not in itself of supreme value. Doubtless; but yet it may be a condition of the goodness of the conduct which it informs. Now the relation of the unity of what is good to the detail which is unified may not be properly compared with the relation of a rule to instances subsumed under it. It is rather comparable with that of a plan, purpose, or design to the detail in which it is carried out. But Kant may be cited in support of the view that unity in a manifold of detail is necessary to the goodness of what is good. For the rest, as realized in divers goods each with different detail, it is no more than a generic factor; and the goodnesses of different such goods differ in kind. And if the rightness of right actions is a form of goodness, then the right actions too may differ from one another in their ways of being right. Good not being a simple quality, we must not expect to find all particular goods so many, or so much, of the qualitatively same. Even a simple quality like yellow is capable of certain variations, in shade, brilliancy, saturation. If goods were yellows, yet the generic identity would not be the whole of what constituted the particulars to be prized for instances of yellowness; the specific differences would be also important. How much more where the unity is not that of simple qualitative identity, but that of unifying a manifold detail. The detail cannot be unimportant, since it makes possible the unity, and different details make possible different forms of unity. The point is, that the elements of detail are not good by virtue of the qualities of the elements considered severally, so that the goodness of the whole that they form should be the aggregate of their separate goodnesses. They are good by virtue of their so suiting one another—which they could not do but for their qualities severally—as to constitute a unified whole which is good. It is not only then the unification that matters, but also what is unified, since the first is only possible through the qualities of the several elements of the second. And if we have established this, has not something been done towards finding a common goodness in different goods, without refusing goodness also to them in virtue of that in which they differ?

Let us now turn to the application of this conception, and consider first the instance of pleasure. We know that some have said that pleasures only are good. But so far is this from being plausible, that it might rather be asked whether pleasure is good at all, by itself. Imagine a world whose only nature it was to consist of beings just sufficiently conscious to feel pleasure; not conscious of one another, nor of anything at which they were pleased. In such a world, there would be no apprehension of what kind of a world it was, nor approval of it for being what it was. Therefore, it could not even be thought good by any mind belonging to it. But let us suppose that a mind not belonging to it were to consider it, and to consider it (for this is important) not as an object of his contemplation; to consider it so would be to treat it as a factor in a more comprehensive whole, to which he also belonged. He might think this whole the better for his having it to contemplate, but that is not the question. The question is, what he could hold it to be by or for itself. And so considered he could not, I think, pronounce it good. For let this pleasure-world cease to be contemplated; would there be any further loss of good in its ceasing to be? Only if there were a loss of something which it itself while it lasted could find good; and this it could not do.

But that the whole nature of the world should lie in feeling pleasure, or in pleasures felt, is, it may be objected, an extravagant imagination. Pleasure occurs in the lives of beings whose lives have much else in them, and who are much more than pleasure-feelers; and those of them who are able to pass judgement on the lives they know recognize pleasure to be a good element in these lives. I should say yes, *in most contexts*. But are there no contexts in which pleasure occurs that are the worse for its presence? A surgeon compelled by his profession, in the days before anaesthetics, to inflict pain on his patients, if he had taken pleasure in watching their pain, would have lived a life the worse for this pleasure, in a world the worse for his feeling it. I do not mean merely that his character would have been bad; that would have been so if he had sought pleasure this way but failed to feel it. I mean that a world where men found, as well as sought, pleasure from inflicting suffering on others would be made worse, not better, by the occurrence of the pleasure sought.

It is the relation of pleasure to the other factors in the whole to which it belongs that settles whether we can call it good or bad; 'in itself' it is not good, but pleasure. So it is with pain; there are pains which enhance the goodness of the wholes in which they occur, like the pain which a man gladly endures in efforts made to help those whom he loves. If a man says that these are not the pleasures and pains of which he is speaking, when he judges pleasure to be good and pain evil, we may well believe him. But we may point out that in so saying he means that he is thinking of pleasures and pains that arise in other contexts and not in those, and in connexion with other circumstances. And if so, he has admitted that he cannot say whether pleasure, nor again whether pain, is good or bad, so long as he considers it in isolation. He was thinking of them in some normal contexts, in which pleasure is good, and pain bad.

Something of the same sort may be said of scents or sounds or colours. There are some whose presence may help to make the goodness of most wholes into which they enter; yet these very sorts may merit condemnation in other contexts. The details constitutive of such unitary wholes as we can judge good because of the natures of these details are themselves good; but not prior to their being in these wholes, unless they are themselves subordinate wholes constituted on the same principle. Then we might find goodness in them without looking beyond them; but our judgement on them might be modified when we considered them as elements along with others in a more comprehensive whole; and it would not be final, nor should we really know, until we could see them in the all-embracing whole.

What then of actions—particular right actions? Actions, it has been argued, which we judge that we ought to do must have some common character to be a ground why we ought to do them. It is not enough to say that we ought to do each on the ground of its own specific nature; our obligations are not a heap of unrelated obligations. This common ground is their rightness, τὸ δίκαιον εἶναι, in that sense of rightness in which to say that an action is right is to assert a character in it, not an obligation on us. And rightness is a sort of goodness. We can say, therefore, that the notion 'right' presupposes the notion 'good'. In the sense that we are obliged, it presupposes it as a consequence its ground; in the sense of what obliges us, as a species its genus.

I do not minimize the difficulty of establishing this position, however great, as I have tried to show, is the alternative difficulty of surrendering it. There is no particular difficulty so long as the right act, which a man ought to do, is the initiation of some changed condition of things, as they enter into men's lives, which has, or will without further act of his bring about what has, a goodness that would be admitted equally to belong to such condition of things if it came about without man's agency. That it may be a man's duty to bring into being, when he has the power to do so, what does not now exist, but would be recognized, if it did exist, to be good, few would be prepared to dispute. But we may well doubt whether, whenever we judge that we ought to do an action, we think that we shall thereby bring into being some good which is not the goodness of our acting, but one for the sake of which we act. The examples which inspire this doubt are perhaps of two main kinds.

Those of the first kind are drawn from the practice of what Hume called the indirect virtues, such as justice, veracity, fidelity to promises. Whereas particular acts of beneficence each produce some new state of affairs that we should judge good if it came about in the course of nature or by chance, particular acts of justice, veracity, fidelity need not. The Utilitarian defence of them, which Hume adopts, is familiar enough. 'They are highly useful', he says, 'or indeed absolutely necessary to the well-being of mankind: but the benefit resulting from them is not the consequence of every individual single act; but arises from the whole scheme or system concurred in by the whole, or the greater part of the society.'[1] The argument is sufficient to show that the observance of them universally is instrumental to a state of things better than if they were not observed at all. It is insufficient to show that it is instrumental to one better than if they were observed or disregarded with an enlightened consideration of the circumstances. For if no benefit, but the reverse, would result from some single act that one of these virtues demanded, and it could be forborne without any weakening of the disposition to practise them generally, a better state of things would result from forbearing it.

Many Utilitarians, for example Henry Sidgwick[2], accept this consequence. Yet it could be pushed to a point where most men would revolt; as that when the good of the state seems to require the discovery and punishment of perpetrators of some baneful and spreading sort of crime, those in authority might secure the arrest and sentence of a man whom they knew to be innocent, provided they were certain that every one else believed and would continue to believe him guilty. It may be said that they could not be quite certain. The objection is irrelevant. This consequence would follow if they could; are we prepared to accept it on that supposition?

[1] *Enquiry concerning Morals*, App. III, § 256.
[2] *Methods of Ethics*, IV. v, § 3.

An example of the second kind occurs when a man judges that he ought to do one rather than another of two actions, the resultant goods to be expected from which appear equal, but would consist, if he acted one way, in his enjoyment of certain advantages; if he acted the other way, in another man's doing so. Here again, there are those who would deny any obligation to prefer the second course of action, and even any goodness in so doing, unless there were a previous obligation towards the other man. But I question whether the general verdict would be that there was no goodness in so doing.

Clearly in neither kind of action which I have illustrated will the instrumental view of rightness apply. Consciousness of obligation to do actions of these sorts is not aroused by apprehension of a greater good to result from them than from the alternative actions considered. Clearly also, as long as we consider such actions by themselves, as pieces or bits of living, if I may use the expression, which a man asks himself whether he ought, or judges that he ought, to enact or live, they will not appear intrinsically good, or intrinsically better than their alternatives; our enacting them for the sake of their intrinsic goodness cannot, we must remember, be the goodness we are looking for as a reason for enacting them. If then we are to find a goodness, for the sake of which to enact them, we must in some way look beyond them: yet not to their *effects*, for we cannot find it there.

I have spoken of pieces or bits of living, though the expression be strange, because I want to keep attention fixed on the fact, already emphasized, that in Ethics we do not mean by action what we do in physical science. Physical science treats all that happens in the world as movements of bodies, which might occur equally if no being knew them, if there were no conscious life. Actions, in any sense in which in such a world men's movements could be called actions, would have no goodness or rightness. Even if they were accompanied by feelings of pleasure, so long as consciousness took no other form than feeling pleasure, there would be no action in the ethical sense, and so no goodness or rightness of action. An action which a man thinks he ought to do is not what physical science can study; and in calling it a piece or bit of living we must not understand living as that with which the biologist is concerned.

If an action then, as a bit of living, as something which a man judges that he ought to include in his life, has an instrumental rightness, like that of doing an extra piece of work from the profits of which he hopes to afford his son a better education, it is the thought of thus securing to his son a better education that moves or obliges him. And if what obliges is the thought of what is right, in that sense of 'right' in which it is a character of the act which a man owes to do, then the act which has this character is the working to secure for his son a better education; though this is because his son's being better educated is independently good. I say the working in order to secure it[1], not being the cause of it, as regular exercise is the cause of good health. If a man had worked with no intention of educating his son, and dying early had left a property from which his heirs had educated the son, the son's being educated would have had as much goodness as if his father had worked to secure it, but the father's work would not. The goodness in the father's working to secure it is simply the goodness of his working with that purpose, not of his acting from a sense of obligation. But in proportion as a man, moved by the thought of the goodness of securing to his son a better education to work with that purpose, is

[1] Cf. *supra*, p. 56, note 1.

opposed by inclinations to take his ease, or otherwise employ himself, the sense of obligation becomes a factor through which he is led to connect the goodness of this action with that of a general plan or system of action, to which the performance of this and other particular actions belongs; and then he acts from a sense of obligation. That, however, is not necessary; and where actions have an instrumental goodness, one need not look beyond their results and them. The instrumental view fails when the acting to secure something is judged good or better, but what is to be secured is not.

So in the case where I debate whether to retain or give to another that, the possession of which by either seems to me equally good, say the means for a much-needed holiday, if I think I ought to give it to another, that must be because my giving it him and not just his having the holiday has a goodness absent from my taking a holiday; for it is my taking it, and not merely my having it, that is the alternative; the having of the holiday by either is equally good. And the difficulty is to see why I should judge my giving it to him better than my taking it for myself, when I judge my having it as good as his having it. *Ex hypothesi*, I am asking which I ought to do, and shall act upon that judgement, so that, whichever I do, I shall have been moved by the thought of the rightness of, i.e. a certain goodness in, the action. Where is this to be found in giving him the holiday more than in taking it? We must not confuse the question with the question whether, looking back, afterwards, I should rather approve myself for having, from a sense of obligation, or it might be from affection, let another enjoy a holiday to my loss, than for having taken it to his loss because I desired it. In that judgement the alternatives compared include differing motives supposed to have determined the alternative courses. But in the judgement which I have to make before action, when I ask which course is right, which do I owe to do, it is assumed that the same motive will have determined me in the adoption of either course; and the determining difference must be a goodness in one course that is not in the other, and which I call its rightness. It is this which is sometimes so difficult to find, even where I judge that I owe to take the one course, and not the other.

It would seem then as if there are some actions which we think we owe to do, or the thought of which obliges us, but in which we apprehend no goodness to make them right, so long as we look only to them; nor can we find it by looking to their effects. If I desired a holiday, and also out of affection for another desired to let him have it instead, though I genuinely believed that his having it and my having it, at the gift of a third party, would be equally good, I might distinguish the alternative uses of my means open to me not by the goodness of their results, but because I thought it intrinsically better, *ceteris paribus*, to act from affection for another than from desire of something to be enjoyed by myself, and so judged that I ought to send my friend on the holiday. But our case is one where I have not that affectionate desire, and so can find greater goodness no more in one alternative *action*, than in its effects. Can I find it if I look at the alternative actions in a wider context, not furnished by their effects? And if so, what is this context? Were it possible to do this, the defence of my original judgement, that I owe to do this action, would lie in the goodness not of it but of the system which it forms with its context; and it would be the thought of the goodness in this system, rather than in the particular action alone, that obliged me.

I would submit that in principle this is possible, however difficult it may be to work out in every case. The point chiefly to be insisted on at the outset is that the context is not composed of the effects, nearer or more remote, of the particular right action; else we should be simply reverting to the instrumental view of rightness, which has broken down. We must look beyond the particular action not to its effects but to the rule of action of which it is a manifestation. This, however, is not enough. We must look to the whole form of life in some community, to which all the actions manifesting this rule would belong, and ask whether it, or some other form of life is better, which would be lived by the community instead, if this rule were not helping to determine it. If we judge that it is better, then the particular action is right, for the sake of the better system to which it belongs. But this system is not the consequence of the particular action, nor the consequence of the working of the rule which requires this action. A form of life is not related to the rules or principles of action that work in it as a consequence to its cause. Also, it is what it is in virtue of the working of other rules in it as well.

The solution here proposed seems to me partly to follow Kant's instruction for determining whether an action is right, that you should act on that principle which you can will should be law universal. In practice that means, that you should ask yourself whether, if it lay with you to effect, you would have all men, in situations such as you have to act in, proceed on the rule on which you propose to proceed; e.g. in the situation of a debtor, put the payment of a debt before other uses of the money which you propose to renounce in order to pay your debt, not from fear of being sued, nor for the sake of the better consequences to ensue from this creditor recovering what he lent, but in consideration of the fact that you had borrowed. But Kant attempts, with how little consistency or success has often been pointed out, to show that by no other rule than that by which in your present situation you judge that you owe to go, could all men go in such situations, without making impossible the actions that the other rule requires; and hence that every other rule is self-contradictory. E.g. you may propose to secure another man's belief of what you know to be false by lying to him; but if all persons proposed that to themselves, whenever they spoke to others, or even only whenever for any reason it suited them, they would cease to believe each other, and so fail to secure by their lying the belief of others in what they said; and this is what they proposed to secure.

I need not labour the criticism that, provided the rule which you take for yourself is less widely formulated, and only covers lying in situations of a detailed description such as rarely occur, though your present situation is such, the adoption of the same rule by others in like situation would not undermine men's confidence in whatever they were told, and, therefore, would not defeat its own purpose. We must drop the pretence that only the rule covering the right action can be universalized without making impossible the actions it covers, though it is true that no action of mine is right, unless it would be right for any one else like me to act thus in a like situation. But if we do drop this pretence, and so can no longer distinguish the unique right action from all others as wrong on the ground that it alone is covered by a rule that can be universalized without self-defeat, then we must look elsewhere for a basis of discrimination. And if we are not to look to the consequences of the particular action proposed, we must look to the form of life requiring the particular action in the working out of its plan. If we find that life better than one which, because it worked out a different plan, would not require the action, then we must accept the particular action with the form of life to which it belongs, and do it not so much for its own sake as for the sake of a goodness in that form of life which the rule requiring this action would determine, if this rule had expression in the lives of others also who make up the community that lives this form of life.

It may be asked, Why have any rule? Why not pay a debt when the consequences of so doing would be better than those of leaving it unpaid, and when the contrary, not pay it? This is the Utilitarian doctrine proper. I do not think that all doctrines should be called Utilitarian, which find the reason why one ought to do an action in some goodness to be realized in or not without doing it. For what consequences can be meant? They may be enjoyments and other good changes to be produced in men's lives, such as some one's receiving a better education than he otherwise might. But they will not include actions of the sort that we are judging right, whether it be that we judge right the paying of a debt or the withholding payment. That cannot be its own consequence; and if we hold that we ought to do it *for the sake of* its consequences, these cannot include acts like it. For the act which has no intrinsic goodness is held right because its consequences have; but if these are acts like it, they can have no intrinsic goodness either, and, therefore, cannot justify the action whose consequences they are. If rabbits are themselves worthless, they cannot be of value as producing rabbits. I think that this, nevertheless, is what the modification amounts to, which Rashdall makes in Sidgwick's Utilitarianism.[1] He agrees with Sidgwick that I can only owe to do an action, or that an action can only be right, because of its consequences; but he complains that Sidgwick has only considered consequences in the way of pleasure, and

[1] *Theory of Good and Evil*, i. 63, 184.

that we ought also to consider consequences in the way of right action. The theory here suggested would, I think, avoid this inconsequence.

Moreover, so long as we justify each action separately by reference to its consequences, even if (with Hume) we include in these the benefits to arise from the other like acts which would not be done if this were not, and so find indirect good consequences to justify an act whose direct consequences alone could not justify it, we are thinking of the good to be realized by men living a common or associated life as an aggregate of particular goods. This is how those Utilitarians most emphatically think of it who define it as the greatest quantity of pleasure with the least admixture of pain. But this aggregate is no one's. Even one man's good is not an aggregate; *a fortiori* the good to be realized in a society cannot be. But the goodness of a form of life in which a principle of action works, and which one may say is animated by it, is not an aggregate. It has that unitary character which we have seen that goodness must have. This, perhaps, is why we naturally think that we ought to act on principle, even while uncertain on what principle we ought to act. To act on principle is to live a life with unity of design in which one act is what it is because of what others are, or were, or will be, and we might as it were read in each act the form of the whole. This is what we demand of a work of art also.

The comparison with a work of art will serve to introduce a not unimportant elucidation of the view here advanced. A rule of action is not quite like the major premise of a syllogism, prescribing that in all situations X one should do Y, and leaving no problem but to recognize instances of X. It is one of the defects of Aristotle's *Ethics*, that he supposes syllogistic thinking to bulk so large in our thinking about what we ought to do. But he 'loved the syllogism as his own work, as well as for its uses, like other men'.[1] Rules of action, as he himself in one place says, have to adapt themselves to the diversities of situations, like a leaden straight-edge.[2] Therefore, what I have said is not inconsistent with admitting that there may be exceptions to going by a rule, which yet men must mostly go by, if the best form of life is to be realized. Morality, says Burke, somewhere in his *Reflections on the French Revolution*, must on occasion suspend its own rules in obedience to its own principles. I do not think this is unintelligible. There are rules of rhythm in verse, which should realize themselves only with constant slight play of variation, if a dead monotony is to be avoided, and from which if on occasion the poet departs further, the poem is better, not worse. The same, I suppose, is true in music. And something like it is what distinguishes response to stimulus in a living thing from that in a machine, if the first is really adaptive; though there are rules of response to stimulus displayed in the form of a living thing's life, yet if because of some peculiarity in the situation the maintenance of the specific form requires some departure from the rule, the response adapts itself accordingly. So it is anyhow in the working of rules in a moral, if not in a physical, life. And therefore, the various rules which men invoke to justify different actions, such as the rules of the Decalogue, are not an aggregate any more than the goodness of a life animated by them is an aggregate. How, if they were, and stood co-ordinate, each obliging unconditionally, should we act in a situation to which two or more applied conflictingly? Hence, as the problem of a particular action drives us to compare the life which would be lived through the working of its rule therein with the life animated by another, so

[1] Cf. Plato, *Rep.* i. 330 c.
[2] *Eth. Nic.* v. x. 7, 1137^{b} 30, μολίβδινος κανών.

the problem of a rule drives us on to consider the life that would be lived, if a more comprehensive form than this rule yields were at work therein, realizing itself sometimes through actions covered by the rule, and sometimes not. It would be the consciousness, however inadequately realized, of this all-embracing form of life, rather than of some single rule, that must really lie at the base of our unmediated judgements about the rightness of particular acts. And this would be what we must make explicit, if we are to defend these judgements to ourselves or others.

IX

THE RIGHT, MY GOOD, AND THE COMMON GOOD

WE may summarize as follows that which the previous discussions have endeavoured to maintain. There is a rightness in right actions distinguishable from our obligation to do them, though the latter is also sometimes meant by calling them right. This rightness is a form of goodness, to the realizing of which the actions belong; and it is the thought of this goodness which moves us when we do an action from a sense of obligation. Further, though the goodnesses of right actions may differ from one another, as they do from those of goods which are not actions, we can yet see a certain common principle of structure in different goods; and in systems of this structure, the goodness of the parts, which may be particular right actions, is not independent of that of the system to which they belong. We recognize an extension of this principle, when we have to decide which of various not compossible goods we or others should endeavour to realize; it is not so much these as certain alternative forms of life to which they would severally belong that we compare.

I wish now to consider a few objections which might be brought against this position, and also its bearing on certain other ethical problems: in particular on the nature of freedom, the nature of obligation, and the question whether the conviction of obligation need be connected in any way (as Plato seems to have thought) with the recognition that my own good is realized in fulfilling it.

Perhaps the most obvious objection is that in fact we do not look so far afield, in judging the actions of others, or determining what we owe to do. We seem to apprehend actions of certain sorts to be right or wrong immediately: that we ought to speak the truth, keep promises, pay debts; that we ought not to be cruel, or cheat. Can we not know all this so soon as we consider any actions of these kinds?

Cruelty at any rate has an intrinsic badness distinguishable from the fact that we ought not to act cruelly. Few judgements are so evidently true as that. But if in considering and condemning a particular act of that sort we see that cruelty is wrong universally, are we not realizing that a form of life in which the principle of the particular action prevailed would be evil? It may be replied that we need not think beyond the particular act. But we cannot understand the particular act except as the expression of a purpose of a certain sort, which implicitly ranges beyond this act. It is not just the pain inflicted that makes the cruel act wrong. Cruelty is inflicting pain on another for its own sake, or for enjoyment of contemplating it. That, perhaps, has never been thought to be a duty, though unhappily it has not always been realized to be wrong. But judicial torture has been thought right, and surgery still is. If any one were asked why cruelty is wrong, he might say, because it causes pain, and pain is evil. But clearly that answer would not suffice. We must look beyond the pain; what we condemn is a 'bit of living' inspired by a certain motive.

Indeed, that there are better and worse motives, without taking into account the sense of duty, is hardly disputed. And I do not contend that judgements of good and evil are never passed on particular actions until we see their relation to everything else; only, that we do, because we see their place in a wider system that we judge good, find a goodness in some which we could not find otherwise; and that it is finding *this* goodness which makes us judge that we ought to do these actions. A man who claims to know his obligation to do a certain action without regard to any good may not easily be refuted directly. But he admits that he ought to do it because it is of a certain *kind*. Herein he has already looked beyond the individuality of the action; and I suggest that where goodness cannot be found in the act to be done, by itself, it may be found in a form of life which cannot be lived except from a principle that requires this act; and that, unconsciously, a man may be aware of this who professes to see the obligation without looking beyond this act, and therefore without looking to anything that he can find good.

Why ought I to keep this promise? Because keeping it is good. Why? Because it is doing what you ought to do. This is to move in a circle. But why ought I to take Paul to see this race? Because you promised, and he will therefore be disappointed if you don't, and you will bring into being his disappointment, which is evil. But Peter will be more disappointed if I do, therefore by keeping it I shall bring more evil into being. But you will also, if you break it, bring the evil of a wrong action into being. Why is the action wrong? We are in the circle again. But let us consider not merely the good or evil of disappointments, and such other items whose good or evil would be the same if they came about through no action of ours. Let us consider two forms of life lived by men together in which goods and evils of this sort are the same, but come about differently: disappointments for example in the one because of broken promises, enjoyments again through the action of men moved by the thought of promises they had made, while in the other these same goods and evils come about not through actions judged wrong or right. These forms of life which men live together, viewed as wholes, are better or worse in respect of how these goods and evils come about, as well as in respect of what they are; and we think this without having to suppose that the particular actions bringing some good about were done from a sense of obligation. It is enough that I should have been moved to take Paul by the consciousness of having promised. But if I now ask whether it is my duty to take him, I can say, the better form of life is the expression of a rule of action, to act by which requires that I should take him, though merely his being taken and Peter disappointed does not seem better than its alternative.

It is difficult to deny that more goes to determine many of our judgements of right and wrong than we are conscious of in making them. It is a familiar observation that acts severely condemned in one form of society are lightly or not at all condemned in another, like refusing hospitality to strangers; and explanations of such facts can be given that connect the wrongness with social conditions which, in an age and country where it is no longer alleged, have passed away. Yet the reasons for these conflicting judgements need not be present to the minds of those confidently making them. Considerations of which men are not explicitly conscious play a large part in determining their judgements in many fields; in none perhaps a larger than in conduct. And unless the mind never works intelligently except with full consciousness of what it is doing, this need not disturb us. But then, might not such considerations as I have suggested play their unrecognized part in a judgement of obligation which seems quite isolated, but can be justified by bringing them to consciousness?

Obligations, I have urged, are not a heap of unconnected obligations. True judgements about right and wrong must somehow connect with one another, not indeed as deductions from some one ultimate major premise, but as each helping to articulate the nature of that system of life or lives to which all actions with which moral judgement is concerned belong, and which more surely than any lesser system within it can be judged good or bad. Nevertheless, we confidently make many moral judgements without going so far; sometimes we claim to know that they are true. Even so, they need not be really independent. The facts of good and evil apprehended separately may yet be connected. It may be as in mathematics. There a man may come to know, independently one of another, many facts between which he later discovers necessary connexion. Indeed in this field it is hard to doubt that all facts are mutually involved, though we cannot show this. Some have urged that, if this is so, the apprehension of the facts in their isolation is not properly to be called knowledge of them; we do not really know anything unless we know it in all its linkages. Perhaps there is a parallel here between Ethics and Mathematics. We think we know of certain actions separately that we ought to do or forbear them. But if the obligation is grounded in some goodness or badness which the action would have, and which is not independent of its being so linked with other actions as to make good or bad the form of life to which it and they would belong, it might be said that we could not really know our obligation till we viewed the action in these linkages. Yet in both fields some isolated judgements seem true, though the facts cannot be so independent of each other as the judgements are isolated.

It may be said that Kant has shown the primacy of the consciousness of obligation, and the absence of any connexion between the knowledge of our duty to do an action and that of any good to be realized by doing it, other than a manifestation of a good will. But this would not be quite accurate. It is true that Kant 'will have nothing to do either with the idea that the rightness of an action depends on its being for our own good, or with the idea that we think of it as so depending, or with the idea that desire for our own good is our only motive'.[1] But that is not the same as holding that its rightness depends in no way on its relation to good. Whether it could really be my duty to do an action, unless by doing it I in some sense realized my good, in the sense perhaps of making what is good mine (and I suggest that it can never be nobody's, though it might be everybody's), I do not at the moment inquire. We are concerned now with the question whether right is conceivable except in relation to good. And I do not think that Kant has shown, or even really thought, that it is.

For in the first place does he not say that 'nothing can possibly be conceived in the world, or even out of it, which can be called good without qualification, except a Good Will?'[2] It is the supreme *bonum*. The actions which it wills are right, but willing and doing them is good. Reflection on the Good Will fills the mind with ever increasing admiration and awe.[3] The moral law reveals to me a *life* of myself independent on animality and even on the whole sensible world, and my *worth* is infinitely elevated by the fact that I have this nature, as an intelligence [4]; a personality in which a good will dwells and works is supremely good.

You may urge that in all this Kant is rather saying that good is inconceivable except in reference to right, than vice versa. But is that really so? Would that not mean that willing the right could be understood without supposing there is anything good, either in the action willed or in its consequences, and that only in reflecting on such

[1] Prof. H. A. Prichard, *Duty and Interest*, p. 44.

[2] *Grundlegung der Metaphysik der Sitten*, p. 11; Hartenstein, iv. 241: *E. T.* (T. K. Abbott), p. 9.

[3] *Kritik der praktischen Vernunft*, Conclusion, p. 312; Hartenstein, v. 167; *E. T.*, p. 260.

[4] *Ib.*, p. 313; Hartenstein, v. 168. (Italics mine.)

willing need we come to conceive anything (to wit, just the willing itself) as good?

Moreover, there is a passage in the *Methodology of Pure Practical Reason* where Kant considers how the 'educators of youth' should proceed, if they wish a boy to feel not only an interest in employing his power of judgement upon moral subjects, but 'an interest even in the law of reason and in morally good actions' [1]:—that means, to care whether he himself is moral or not. They should tell him, e.g., the history of an honest man whom men want to persuade to join the calumniators of an innocent and powerless person: whom they first tempt with bribes and then threaten with loss, of friendship, fortune, freedom, life: whose dearest connexions also they threaten, so that these entreat him to yield and he wishes 'that he had never seen the day that exposes him to such unutterable anguish', yet remains 'true to his upright purpose, without wavering or even doubting'. 'Then', says Kant, 'will my youthful hearer be raised gradually from approval to admiration, from that to amazement, and finally to the greatest veneration, and *a lively wish that he himself could be such a man* (though certainly not in such circumstances). Yet virtue is here worth so much only because it costs so much, not because it brings any profit.' [2] 'All the admiration, and even the endeavour to resemble this character, rest wholly on the purity of the moral principle.'

Surely the meaning of this is that the way to make a boy care to act rightly is to make him realize how *good* it is to be one who so acts. 'This is the happy Warrior; this is He That every Man in arms *should wish to be*.' But to act rightly is to live your life in a certain way. And even the

---

[1] Op. cit., p. 310; Hartenstein, v. 165; *E. T.*, p. 258.

[2] Ib., p. 305; Hartenstein, v. 161, 162; *E. T.*, p. 254. (Italics mine.)

happiness of man is a living in a certain way. It is this even if it consists in pleasure and the absence of pain. On any view of happiness, it must be an activity of soul, ἐνέρ-γεια ψυχῆς, even if of a soul that can only feel. An interest in morality itself is therefore an interest in being oneself moral, though it does not exclude an interest in others being so too; and that interest cannot be ultimately separated from the conviction that one's own good lies in being so. And if one asks why, the answer must be that to be moral is to be actuated by a principle which, working in one's life, makes it good; or at least does more towards making it good than any other one factor can. For Kant held, and perhaps correctly, that the good will working in a life does not of itself suffice to make that life as good as a life can be. The *supremum bonum* is not the *summum bonum*.

This is really in no way inconsistent with his statement that 'virtue is here worth so much only because it costs so much, not because it brings any profit'. He does not think that its costing so much constitutes its worth. If I am pre-pared to pay much in order to retain that from which I expect nothing, it is because what I retain is itself precious to me. What it costs me is mere evidence of its intrinsic worth in my eyes. According to Kant, a will acting under a sense of duty is not better than a holy will, though to human perception the ideal of such a will (as offered us in the example quoted) 'seems to cast in the shade even *holiness* itself, which is never tempted to transgression. This, however, is an illusion arising from the fact that as we have no measure for the degree of strength except the greatness of the obstacles which might have been over-come (which in our case are the inclinations), we are led to mistake the subjective conditions of estimation of a magnitude for the objective conditions of the magnitude in itself'.[1] Virtue, he says, is its own end; and by virtue he means acting morally, or from respect for the law. But of course the relation of means and end cannot really hold between anything and itself, and the phrase only signifies that it is intrinsically good. Acting morally, however, as we have seen, cannot be merely realizing self-consistency in one's actions; it is living a life according to a certain form, only realized in it if it is actuated or animated by certain rules or principles, of which that form needs the observance in the activities which realize it; though these activities involve also a number of particular desires. The realization of this form of life may require that all sorts of inclinations, if we have them, go ungratified; therefore, there may be obstacles to be overcome. But many other ends which men set before them, called by Kant 'human ends', have their obstacles to be overcome. Only, he says, the worth of virtue 'far outweighs that of all empirical ends and advantages which it may have as consequences'.[2] He is certainly not arguing that we need to be convinced of this in order to know that we ought to live virtuously. But in the answer to the question πότερον λυσιτελέστερον ἀδικία δικαιοσύνης, or whether injustice profits a man more than justice, it is difficult to see any difference between what he says here and what Plato taught, if it be remembered that λυσιτελεῖν need not mean to bring a profit that is distinct from what brings it, and has the worth which what brings it has not. After all, on this issue at any rate, Aristotle did not dissent from Plato; he said that acting well was the end of action, whether or not that was consistent with saying that every action seems to *aim at* some end. That man acts virtuously who does what he does for its nobility, τοῦ καλοῦ ἕνεκα, and the καλόν is the worth in what he does.

---

[1] *Metaphysische Anfangsgründe der Tugendlehre*, p. 244; Hartenstein, vii. 200; *E. T.*, p. 308.   [2] Ib.

In these last remarks I have not kept altogether distinct the questions whether our duty is to realize what is good, and whether in doing so we realize our own good. I do not think they can be separated, if it is true that the good is living a certain form of life: by which I mean, that the real, if it is good, must be a spiritual system, not a physical system which, even if it be known, could equally exist unknown. The whole consisting of a physical system and minds aware of it might be called good, so long as it is not conceived as two independently good things thrown together, minds equally good though they were aware of anything else or nothing at all, and a physical world equally good though no mind were aware of it. We may indeed call that good which we think capable of the right form of life, though it be not actualizing its capacity; as Aristotle said that our virtues, though not our happiness, are ours in sleep. But all capacities are denominated from that of which they are the capacities, and a capacity is only good from the goodness of its actualization.

Mr. E. F. Carritt [1] says that 'what we . . . immediately judge right is always doubtless the bringing about of some state of things. But the state we ought to bring about is not first judged to be best in any other sense than that it is the one we ought to bring about. If it came about by chance or necessity, we should not always judge it specially good.' And he proceeds to give examples like those taken above to show that a goodness cannot always be found in the action which we judge right, considered by itself, or in that action's consequences. But if it can be found in a form of life impossible to realize except through a principle which involves doing that action, then this form of life is what we ought to bring about; and a form of life can only come about in living it. Here 'life' means a

[1] *Theory of Morals*, § 64, p. 72.

spiritual, not a physical, activity, and so is something which cannot come about by chance or necessity.

Now if *that* is the good which *I* ought to bring about, it is realized, partly at least, in *my* living it. How it can be mine and yet good absolutely we can perhaps understand if we consider, as shall shortly be done, the notion of a common good. It has been suggested that this phrase involves a contradiction in terms.[1] I do not know why. It might be because good can be nobody's, or because if mine it cannot also be another's; but neither statement would seem to me true. Professor Moore, as we saw, thinks that what is good is good whether anybody's or not. 'What is meant', he asks, 'by "my own good"? In what sense can a thing be good for me? It is obvious, if we reflect, that the only thing which can belong to me, which can be *mine*, is something which is good, and not the fact that it is good. When, therefore, I talk of anything that I get as "my own good" I must mean either that the thing I get is good, or that my possessing it is good. In both cases, it is only the thing or the possession of it which is *mine*, not *the goodness* of that thing or that possession.'[2]

Professor Moore seems here to identify the goodness of a thing with the fact that it is good, for the statement that something which is good and not the fact that it is good can be mine is repeated in the form that only the thing is mine and not the goodness of it. But I suppose we mean by the goodness of a thing the character or nature in virtue of which we call it good; *denominatur bonum a bonitate*. Its goodness, according to Professor Moore, is a simple and unanalysable quality; the fact that it is good cannot be that; it is not the quality, but the inherence of the quality in the thing. Sometimes, no doubt, by the goodness of a thing

[1] Prof. H. A. Prichard, *Duty and Interest*, p. 33.
[2] *Principia Ethica*, § 59, p. 98. (Italics Professor Moore's.)

we might mean this (allowing for the moment that goodness is a quality). I might say that I had only lately become aware of the goodness of aesthetic enjoyment, though I had long known the goodness of personal affection. Professor Moore holds that there is no difference between them; they are two instances of the same simple unanalysable quality. Therefore, so far as being aware of goodness is concerned, I should have learnt nothing fresh, but I should have learnt its presence in aesthetic enjoyment. The difference is like that between knowing Jones and knowing where he is to be found. Say he is in Honolulu. He is not his presence in Honolulu, and, of course, if he is in Honolulu, his being there is not mine, even were Honolulu mine. It might be called a relation of him to Honolulu, whereas the other is a relation of Honolulu to me. But if his relation to Honolulu were like that of goodness to a good thing, then if he were in Honolulu he would be mine as much as Honolulu was—*adscriptus glebae*, as its goodness is ascribed to the good. Surely it is nonsense to talk as if a thing could be mine without its qualities. I allow that the qualities of what is mine are not qualities of me, when what is mine is some material thing, the possession of which is really a legal right to make use of it. But strictly my good is never a material thing.

The man who says that his good consists 'in the multitude of his possessions' means 'in his possessing a multitude of things'. He probably means that to possess a multitude of things is what he desires, and takes pleasure in bringing about and contemplating. If that is all, he ought to say that what he likes, or what he wants, is to possess a multitude of things; and when I say that something is good for me, I may only mean that it produces a condition of myself which I like or want. Properly, however, I should mean more than this. If it is true that my good lies in possessing

a multitude of things, then my possessing them is good, as
Professor Moore says. But that is not all: at least not if the
good is living a certain form of life, or is a spiritual system.
Its being so would not preclude our allowing that beautiful
things are good; it would only require us to admit that
they are not good except as the work of or object of contemplation to a mind. As such they belong to some form
of life, for life is not doing *in vacuo*. If, then, my possessing
a multitude of things were good, my life would be good
because lived in the consciousness and exercise of my
rights to use them. And if something good is realized in
or constitutes my life, I cannot conceive why it is not mine.
It is mine much more intimately than any *thing* can be. I
agree that what is good is good absolutely; but that does
not prevent it being mine, if it is in me as the form of my
life is in me. What is true is true absolutely; it is also some
opinion or belief; may not that be mine? Is not the truth
mine, if it is I who think truly?

I should be more disposed in this matter to agree with
T. H. Green, when he writes that 'anything conceived as
good in such a way that the agent acts for the sake of it,
must be conceived as *his own* good, though he may conceive it as his own good only on account of his interest in
others, and in spite of any amount of suffering on his own
part incidental to its attainment'.[1]   But that too may be
misunderstood.

How it should be understood may best be seen by considering the notion of a common good. Mr. Carritt says [2]
that 'a common good may mean either (1) some act which
all members of a group agree in thinking ought to be done,
or (2) something from whose use they all may derive
satisfaction, or (3) some state of things which they all
desire should be brought about'. I think we may for

[1] *Prolegomena to Ethics*, § 92.   [2] *Theory of Morals*, § 78, p. 99.

present purposes omit sense (2), which is rather that of 'useful'. But the common good, as I understand it, would include instances of (1) and (3). If what is good is a form of life, a common good is a form of life lived in common; and we must ask what that would be. Now we can share one another's lives only through knowledge and sympathy, through desiring and knowing that we desire the same things, through thinking and knowing that we think that the same acts ought to be done. *Idem velle et nolle* is necessary, but also to know it of one another. This, however, will not prevent our doing different things, and getting each his enjoyment from doing what another does not do, and therefore does not get *his* enjoyment from doing. These enjoyments will not be common, but the knowledge that they are enjoyed by X and the desire that they should be may be common to X with others. It is true that X's desire to enjoy differs from Y's desire that X should enjoy, but not otherwise than Y's desire to enjoy differs from X's desire that Y should. Now X and Y and others might work with a single (or common) purpose for the realization of a state of things in realizing which they played different parts, yet each in consciousness of what parts the others were playing. They must, of course, have desires for various things; and though some of their desires might be for the same thing, as if a number of men desired that a certain landscape should be preserved from spoliation, or that some one not of their number should be rescued from poverty, others no doubt could not be. X's hunger is a desire that he, X, should eat; Y's that he, Y, should. That, however, does not prevent each desiring that the rest should get what they severally want for themselves and cannot share the enjoyment of with others, as well as desiring what is really the same. For we must remember that a man desires primarily that something should be, and not the satisfaction to be had by him from the coming to be of what he desires. The latter no doubt is private, but not the former.

But the common good which is a form of common life cannot consist in each living only for others: in desiring and endeavouring only that others should accomplish their desires and endeavours. 'For', as Kant says, 'that one should sacrifice his own happiness, his true wants, in order to promote those of others, would be a self-contradictory maxim if made a universal law.'[1] We must suppose then men in divers relations of special intimacy, with divers capacities and desires and needs, getting from these—their exercise or fulfilment—pleasures and satisfactions which others do not. Yet if all this were worked out under the inspiration of principles, or of a purpose towards a certain form of life or combination of mutually adjusted lives, to the realization of which all postponed the gratification of desires which could not be gratified without injury to its realization: if they were not only conscious of this purpose, but of its animating them all: and if it were such a form of life as, because better than any other that they could live together, they recognized they ought to live, so far as in each lay: if further they succeeded in desiring rather that this which they judged good, or best, should be realized than to get such things for themselves as that in them craved which was not wholly conformed to this common purpose: once more, if each not only understood the good-ness of this form of common life, and the obligation on him to set it forward, but had affections of benevolence and love towards others, so as to desire their getting things which they—those others—desired that themselves should

---

[1] Preface to *Metaphysische Anfangsgründe der Tugendlehre*, p. 240; Hartenstein, vii. 197; *E. T.*, p. 304. Cf. Bosanquet, *Some Suggestions in Ethics*, ch. i.

get: then, as it seems to me, they would make their lives good in working together to set forward that common life which they lived in the inspiration of a common purpose; each man's life would be good not independently of and prior to the rest, but through and as belonging to the realization of their common purpose. The goodness of this common life would be the unitary goodness of the whole system; it would consist in these lives lived together. And because each sought to realize his own-life (a system within the one whole system) not just for itself and without looking beyond it, but as being what the whole system required whose realization he desired, and towards which his purpose in living his own life worked, since the purpose towards the whole determined what form the contributory systems should take—because of this the goodness of the whole would be present in the goodness of each man's life; it would be his not exactly in the same way as, yet not less truly than, the goodness of his own life would be his; and it would, therefore, be a common good. It is for this reason that what a man conceives as good in such a way that he acts for the sake of it, though it be nothing which is his own in the sense in which the loss of those dear to him is his loss, and not another's who yet may sympathize with him, or in which his successes are his own, and not another's who yet may most genuinely congratulate him, can yet be *his own* good.

X

DUTY, DESIRE, AND FREEDOM

IT appeared, by what was said at the end of the last chapter, that a man who, under a sense of duty, acts for the sake of what he conceives to be good may in a true sense be said both to act from desire, and from a desire of his own good. But both statements can be misinterpreted, and so disputed. First, does he act at all from desire? Two reasons at least might at once suggest themselves for denying it: (1) that a man acting under a sense of duty is often acting contrary to all his desires, (2) that since a man is, as has been pointed out, responsible for his actions, but not for his desires, except so far as by his actions he can modify these, therefore, if in acting from a sense of duty we act from desire, we do not act freely.

As to (1), a man can want to do something because he thinks that he ought to do it, at a time when he feels no desire with whose gratification doing it would conflict; and even if he feels such a desire, on realizing that to gratify it would prevent him from doing what he thinks he ought, he may lose the desire. That, I suppose, is the experience of those whom Wordsworth, in his *Ode to Duty*, describes as 'Glad hearts, without reproach or blot, Who do thy work and know it not'. It implies that there may be a desire to do what is right as such. I do not, however, think that a man who thus desires to do something *in particular* which he thinks he ought to do need have consciously generalized the ground of his consequent action, so as in doing it to be looking beyond it to a life passed in fulfilment of duty, whereto this action is to belong as a constituent. On the other hand he may have passed from a stage at which, as each action seems a duty, he desires to do it to one at which he sets the fulfilment of duty before him as what he wants to achieve; we say often, the goal of his life, but we should say, the life he wants to live. Now if one can both want to do something in particular because it is one's duty, and also want to live one's life in the discharge of duties as they arise, it would seem that in acting from a sense of duty (as one would be doing in these cases) one may be acting from desire; only that the desire involved differs fundamentally from those desires of whose opposition one is often so acutely conscious when aware of an urgent duty. If this difference is not realized, it is easy to think that we do not act from any desire in acting from a sense of duty: (it might, however, perhaps be more appropriate sometimes to speak of the urgency of the thought of a certain way of acting or living, than of a desire so to act or live).

We may start from what seems the most obvious difference, that in one case a man desires to do something because he ought, in the other he just desires to do, or get, or enjoy something with no 'because' attached, or at least with no *such* 'because'. I may desire to possess a certain book because it is a first edition. But being a first edition is a character of the book in a way in which being what I ought now to do is not a character of answering a letter. If the main contention of these chapters is true, the character of being what I ought now to do belongs to a particular action in virtue of the animating or generating principle of the form of life to the realization of which doing it would belong; but the character of being a first edition belongs to a book just as this book. This difference may be illustrated by an example which, if imaginative, is perhaps not wholly fanciful.

Let me assume that the mechanical interpretation of organic life is mistaken, and that the growth of every organism is the working out of a purpose. If the purpose is not that of the organism itself, we may, not without precedent, personify nature, and think of Nature as carrying out her designs in the individuals of each species. The individuals of one species are so much alike that we may further compare producing them to the various particular actions of a man ascribed to one instinctive desire. The existence of each species in its members corresponds to that of each instinctive desire in its characteristic instances or manifestations. The species, in distinction from its members, may be held to exist either as their common character or as a determinate urge in Nature to the production of its members; just as the instinctive desire may be thought of as a determinate urge in the soul to perform actions of a definite sort, which we group together in referring them to one instinct. On such a view what is called in biology the struggle for existence would be comparable to a struggle of particular desires in a man's soul. For the struggle for existence is carried out between individuals of species, not between species. Only if a brown rat kills a black rat, or gets the food which, if it gets, the black rat will starve, or what not, every time, will the brown species suppress the black; just as only if, every time that I both want to read a book, and want to be doing something else, the other desire is stronger than the desire to read, will reading be exterminated from my life as a species from the fauna of Nature.

Now if this were all, though there would be purpose in the production of each organism, as in attaining through appropriate means the object of any particular desire, there would be none in the struggle for existence, as there would be none in the conflict of two instinctive desires. There would only be an issue to the struggle. And in this case, there would be an evolution of individual organisms, but no evolution of species, though it might be that some of these specific urges in Nature might suppress others, and some species disappear from the world of individuals in consequence. For the term evolution is ill chosen to describe the course of a struggle whose issue is in no way purposed. If on the other hand the gradual replacement of some species by others in the world as time goes on were not accidental, i.e. unpurposed, and a mere result of individual struggles, but due to Nature's preference for what she substituted, we must conceive her approval of one species above another as operative to determine its suppression of the other in a way in which the mere struggle for existence could not be. (If her approval were well grounded, we might also call the more successful species the higher.) For we cannot regard the influence of Nature's approval of a species as the influence of the species approved. The species works through its individuals in their competition with individuals of other species. Their efforts are the urge in Nature of a particular species to maintain itself, like the urge of a particular instinctive desire in a man's soul. The influence of Nature's approval of a species we may, if we like, call the working of the superiority of the species approved, though the being better would be a more appropriate expression; for 'superiority' is a term apt to suggest the result rather than the cause of it. But this superiority, or being better, is neither one of the features of the species, nor its success in the struggle. It is not one of the features of the species, because these would be the same, whatever the other species were, but it would not. It is not the success of the species, because that is just the issue of the competition of its individuals with those of other species, whereas its being better is something influencing the issue of those struggles. We may say that the species is better in virtue of what its features, or rather the features of its individuals, are. But that does not mean that because of them its individuals compete successfully against those of others in the struggle for existence; for then its being better would only be a greater power of self-maintenance; being better, or superior, would *be* being stronger; might would be right, and the approval of Nature would not be required; whereas by the superiority in question we mean something in spite of which, without Nature's approval of it, the superior species might go under in its struggle against inferior, though somehow because of her approval it triumphs.

Though, therefore, we might call the influence of Nature's approval of a species that of its superiority, the superiority can work only through Nature's judgement that it is superior determining her to work in letting her urgency to produce individuals of this species take precedence of the urgencies to produce individuals of other species, in a way quite different from that in which she might be said to work in each particular urgency. So far as these urgencies are concerned, we may, because Nature acts from a different urgency in each of them, say alternatively that a different specific form is urgent in each towards its own manifestation in individuals. But in regard to the urgency in Nature to act upon her judgement of which species are better, we cannot say alternatively that any specific form is here urgent, but only that a form of combination and succession of these specific forms is urgent to establish itself in the distribution of a fauna and a flora that results in the course of the evolutionary struggle.

Now there is the same sort of difference between the urgency of a particular desire or inclination which a man feels in himself who collects first editions, and so desires on hearing of it to possess some fresh example (as the urge of a species expressed itself constantly in organizing the growth of new individuals), and the urgency of the desire to do an action because it is right. Its being right is its being not what a particular impulse or desire would make it, but what the form of the life to which it must belong would make it. The difference is as great as that between some part of an arabesque being what a stencil would make it, and what the beauty of the design to which it belongs requires that it should be. My being moved to act by the apprehended rightness, or by the apprehension of the rightness, of an action is the urgency in me to realize a certain form of life, not the urgency to give expression in act to a desire or impulse of a particular sort. And there are two further points to notice here.

(a) This urgency may work in me with more or with less explicit consciousness of what the form of life is towards which I move. The less conscious of it I am, the less can I say why I ought to do this action, or in what the goodness lies which makes me call it right; the less also shall I seem to myself to be moved by anything which I can call a desire. For desires are known by that towards the realization of which they move us, and which we call their object, and the less we know in advance what that is, the harder it is to recognize our desires. It is, however, also true, though less noticeable, that our particular impulses may move us with more or with less explicit consciousness of what that is towards which they move us, so that we may sometimes find with surprise that we have done something which we did not even know we wanted to do. And I understand that in 'pathological' cases the doing may be fully conscious, and yet a man would not say that he had desired to do what he did; a kleptomaniac, for example, might steal, knowing what he was trying to take, and would even say that he had felt he must, or was in some sense obliged, yet if you asked him why he had done it, he could give no such answer as could be given for normal theft. But this would not have been moral obligation, because he was not moved by the apprehended goodness of what he felt obliged to do, or of a form of life requiring it. Only an impulse to a particular action was working in him, against which other impulses may compete with more or less success in virtue of their relative strengths, not an impulse towards something universal, which moulds to itself the actions towards which our particular impulses move us, so as to make them in divers ways other than what in virtue of these impulses alone they would be, or even to prevent them altogether.

(b) It has been held that there are in men certain definitely bad impulses. If so, it is doubtful whether, in our imagination of a purposive Nature, there is anything corresponding. It would require us to ascribe to her impulses to realize specific forms, all the individuals of which she would nevertheless disapprove. This seems perverse. We might perhaps say that the impulse to produce individuals of a species whose existence at one stage of the evolutionary process she approves might persist into a time when she disapproves their continued occurrence, so that she has not yet exterminated them. Plato and Aristotle spoke of certain lawless or bestial appetites, παράνομοι ἐπιθυμίαι, or θηριώδεις[1], the indulgence of which at any time or in any degree was bad, and which in decent men did not come to consciousness unless (Plato said) in dreams. But, perhaps, even these are not specifically different impulses, but directions of some impulse, which also prompts to acts of which we can approve, into manifestations that can fit into no good form of life. Even cannibalism might be a misdirection of hunger. How-

[1] *Rep.* ix. 571 B; *Eth. Nic.* VII. v. 2, 1148^{b} 19.

ever this be, I mention the matter, because the more completely that towards which the urge of a particular impulse moves us is irreconcilable, even through modification, with the form of life which we approve, the more coercive will our disapproval feel, and the more noticeable in regard to it our sense of obligation to forbear.

There is then a difference of character between a particular desire, which is an urge towards this or that action of a determinate kind, and the urgency belonging to the thought that some action is right. For this is towards not a particular action, but the realization of a certain form of life through particular actions now of one sort and now of another, but for the moment through that which I think I ought to do here and now. A man then acting under a sense of duty may be acting against all his present particular desires, but not on that account without desire; though the desire involved in the thought that an act is right is different in kind from these, and, if only to become effective at their expense, gives rise to the sense of obligation.

(2) The second objection anticipated to the statement, that a man acting under a sense of duty may be also acting from desire, was that it was inconsistent with freedom. For I cannot desire at will. My desires are part of my nature. 'If I believed', writes Mr. Carritt [1], 'that men act as they do because their nature is what it is, I could doubtless distinguish useful from noxious actions, and also those whose contemplation gave me a quasi-aesthetic satisfaction from those which did not; but it is not clear to me that I could form the conception of right, that is, obligatory acts.' 'To suppose', he adds in the next section, 'that, between alternatives which are absolutely determined, we exercise, whenever we recognize a duty, a choice which is absolutely spontaneous, seems to me the hypothesis best fitted to

[1] *Theory of Morals*, § 100, p. 130.

explain the moral experience. And it is no more opposed to science than is any other theory which distinguishes *actions* from events. It is also the hypothesis most consonant with the evidence of introspection.'

I agree that any theory which distinguishes actions from events must be opposed to science in the sense of denying that every change in things can be explained scientifically. But I do not think that to be freely done is to be uncaused. I can hardly expect to contribute anything to the solution of so old and famous and difficult a problem as the freedom of the will. I will only try to put briefly my own view.

That my choice, then, is free does not mean that it does not proceed from what I am, or from my nature. It means that what I am is not to be explained from the nature of something else acting on me, nor from the natures of elements now composing me, which these elements had before entering into the composition which is I, and retain although from time to time they vary their combinations in different aggregates. For then these elements would be the genuine unities, whereas it must be I that am, if the choice is mine. And I do not see why I cannot be called good or bad for being what I am. The reason why we do not praise or blame a pianoforte as we do a man is that its excellences or defects are due to the materials, the maker and the pianist, rather than to it.

It may be asked why, if this is all, we regard intellectual and moral excellence so differently. I am not sure that I can give a wholly satisfactory answer, but one may observe this. There is, I think, between knowledge and moral action the following not unimportant analogy. In moral action we are moved by the thought of a common good; but the common good, if realized, must bring to each man not only the satisfaction of his desire that it should be realized, but the satisfaction of his private interests and desires, which are not those of another man. So in knowledge, so far as men know the world, it is a common object; but it becomes known to them through their fragmentarily perceiving it, and so far as they perceive it, it appears more or less differently to each. We distinguish however between perceiving and knowing even that portion of the common world that comes within our own experience. And it is doubtful whether we should say that knowledge of this common world could not be completely actualized, so long as there is any part of it not by somebody perceived. Again, so little does a man's intellectual excellence depend on any individuality in his intelligence whereby it differs from another man's who is equally intelligent, that the more nearly we know, the less our minds differ; and some one has observed that, instead of saying 'I think', I might more correctly say 'It thinks in me'.

On the other hand, the common good is something which only exists in and through action. Therefore it is necessary that in some individual life everything should be actualized which belongs to or helps to constitute that one form of good life which men living together conceive and desire in common. The realization for any one of that common good, whereof only a small part can be his in the way in which it is no one else's, does demand that all the rest should be some one's in this way; though the knowledge by any one of that common world, whereof only a small part can appear to him through perception in the way in which it appears to no one else, does not demand that all the rest should appear to some one in this way. And a man's moral excellence demands that he should make a special contribution to the actualization of the common good, by the moulding to its requirements of his

S

inclinations and desires, which are not the inclinations and desires that another man must mould into conformity with the same. In respect, therefore, of their moral excellence men must differ one from another, in spite of their agreeing so far as all act from a sense of the obligation that the same form of common life lays upon them to mould to it their several inclinations and desires. But in respect of their intellectual excellence, men would only agree.

Now if we think of spirit in the universe as differentiating itself into finite spirits, then so far as its nature as intelligence is what shows itself in these finite spirits, the difference of finite individual from individual is numerical only; and the credit or praise for intellectual excellence actualized in B seems hardly due to B in particular, since the very same excellence may be actualized in A. If B is to exist as well as A, no doubt it is good that he too should display this intellectual excellence; but it is not necessary to the actualization of intellectual excellence that it should be actualized twice. B, therefore, makes no unique contribution. On the other hand, to the actualization of moral excellence through the living of a perfect form of common life it is necessary that B should do what is right for his part, as well as A for his. Each is a unique manifestation of spirit not only as numerically different from the other, but as different in the nature of its manifestation. And if, as has been held, numerical differentiation would otherwise be impossible, then perhaps the numerical differentiation of the manifestations of the same intellectual excellence is made possible through their union not only with differences in perceptual experience but also with differences of kind between the manifestations of moral excellence. Thus in respect of their moral natures, though they were equally good, A and B must yet differ. One could not replace the other; neither is in any sense superfluous;

the credit or praise, therefore, for any good that either contributes to the realization of the one all-inclusive good is his only; and equally with the blame.

How it is that the thought of the goodness of a certain action, or of a form of life to be set forward by it, moves a man to forgo or modify the indulgence which he would otherwise give to some private inclination or desire, we cannot (as has been seen) explain in terms of a conflict between particular desires of different strengths, nor by any analogies drawn from the explanations familiar in physical science. It presupposes, as even Kant admits, a 'moral feeling'. 'Every determination of the elective will', he says—the will, that is, that chooses—'proceeds *from* the idea of the possible action, *through* the feeling of pleasure or displeasure in taking an interest in it or its effect *to* the deed; and here the *sensitive* state (the affection of the internal sense) is either a *pathological* or a *moral* feeling. The former is the feeling that precedes the idea of the law, the latter that which can only follow': so that the moral feeling is 'the susceptibility to pleasure or displeasure merely from the consciousness of the agreement or disagreement of our action with the law of duty'. 'Now it cannot be a duty to have a moral feeling, or to acquire it; for all consciousness of obligation supposes this feeling in order that one may become conscious of the necessitation that lies in the notion of duty; but every man (as a moral being) has it originally in himself. . . . No man is wholly destitute of moral feeling, for if he were totally unsusceptible to this sensation he would be morally dead.'[1] This seems to come very close to an admission of a desire to do what is right as such, with the proviso that the desire is not excited by the thought of pleasure, as Kant thought all

[1] Preface to *Metaphysische Anfangsgründe der Tugendlehre*, pp. 246–7; Hartenstein, vii. 203; *E. T.*, p. 310.

desires to be, and therefore refused to allow in so many words a desire to do one's duty. And if to do what is right is to realize so far as lies in one's power at the moment a form of good life, and the very conception of this is only possible to us as intelligent beings, not as moved by this or that *particular* interest or desire or instinct (even though there were some fixed number of fundamental instincts in us), then Kant after all, at least in this and some other of his statements, is not so far from agreeing with Plato's doctrine of the part played in the life of the just soul by the rational factor, τὸ λογιστικόν; for that, too, as Plato thought, engages our interest in the good which it enables us to conceive and approve.

The conception of freedom which I have defended in opposition to one that refuses to connect a man's free choice with his nature being what it is may perhaps determine the view that is to be taken in regard to this difficulty, that whereas on the one hand we think a man ought to do what *is* right, on the other we say that an action done from a sense of duty is moral: so that if, because he mistakenly *thinks* it right, and, therefore, from a sense of duty, he does what is not right, he acts morally in doing what is wrong. It is not error about particular matters of fact which raises a problem here. Ignorance of these, as Aristotle long ago pointed out, excuses, if not itself due to moral defect. The error in question is about what is good and evil, better and worse, in those changes in the form of a life which it lies in a man's power to produce. If to act from a sense of duty is to be moved by the thought of a form of good life which requires for its realization the particular action which is *his* duty at the moment, then so far as a man mistakes what he ought to do, he is mistaken about the form of the good life. Now if moral excellence in a finite spirit arises when there is developed in it such a mind and will as would, *pro suo posse*, realize this form, then whether a man fails because he misconceives the good so far as concerns the contribution which he could now make thereto, or because the thought of it does not determine his action, he is defective in his moral nature, and so not free from blame.

We have now defended against both the objections that suggested themselves to it the thesis that a man who, under a sense of duty, acts for the sake of what he conceives to be good is acting from desire. Can he also be acting from a desire of his own good? I should reply yes. The good is a form of common life. Fundamentally, rational action is like artistic creation, which indeed must be a species of it: it is action in which the form to be realized through it moves the agent in the particulars of his activity. A living spirit who in such action realizes *pro suo posse* the form of life which is the real good realizes it in his life, and so creates the good in himself. What is good becomes his, and his good. So far as he is conscious of that towards which the urgency of this form of life is moving him, and conscious of it as not yet realized, he desires its realization. So far as he is conscious of this form of life as involving a certain life of his own in contribution to a form of wider life including his, but realized only in a many lives inspired by a common purpose, he desires to live thus himself, and therefore condemns, if he feels them, any conflicting interests and desires, as urging him towards what is not good; while the life, towards the living of which he is urged by the thought that the form of life including it is good, itself appears through this as good, and as what he desires for himself: and therefore as his good.

But an unquestionable difficulty forces itself upon our attention when we turn from theory to practice. Perhaps it is not only when we turn from this theory to practice that it meets us. All that has been said about a form of common life is more or less easily illustrated, so long as we take a family or some other *small* society as the community in whose lives together this life is to be realized. It is not hard to think of a man really and willingly subordinating the gratification of his private desires to the realization of a good that is to be realized in the lives of those composing this society: not even if it involves his accepting death. But the larger the community, the harder it is to think out how a form of good life may be devised that shall give to the private desires of each such satisfaction as will make the whole seem to resolve itself into, and be the unity of, the lives of all its members, in each of which it dictates some partial and particular form of good life. That a family or other small society may convince themselves that there is no real conflict of interests among them, if only each truly conceives his own, is not incredible, for experience shows it to occur. In a great nation it is already far harder, though at moments of stress and danger and of exaltation of spirit it happens up to a point. But if we take the whole world, when it comes to a question, say upon the failure of harvest over some wide area, which shall suffer, the inhabitants there by starvation, or those of a fertile neighbourhood by the sword, or by starving instead, can we really say that there is a way of settling the issue, if they could only on both sides conceive it, which is at once absolutely good, and makes something good of the lives which it allows to both populations?

That it is expedient that one man should die for the people, both the people and that one man himself have at times equally believed, and believed that thereby the best is realized for both. That it is expedient that one people should perish for another, or for the world, no people has ever yet believed, if it was they that must perish. It is hard to see how a whole people could so believe, unless they were all inspired with that heroic kind of virtue, with which sometimes one man is inspired who genuinely finds his life best when he sacrifices in the interest of others all gratification of his own particular interests and desires, and even life itself. Yet if all conflict of interests is to be resolved, not by force and the defeat of the weaker, but on principles of right, there ought to be a good absolute, the form of which would determine what the lives of all in the common world should be; and all of us, so far as we had understanding and good will, ought to acquiesce in the goodness of this form of life that includes the lives of all, and to desire its realization, however much, in the vulgar judgement, this were to our own hindrance.

And the reader may reject all that has been put forward in this book of positive theory; but he will still have this problem to solve, if he holds that good will and intelligence can settle all disputes between nations in the true interests of all.

INDEX

is anything "good in itself" except goodness?